Copyright Law: A Practical Guide

Victor D. López, J.D., Esq.
Professor of Legal Studies
Hofstra University
Frank G. Zarb School of Business
Hempstead, NY 11549

Copyright Victor D. López 2014, 2018

No portion of this copyrighted book may be copied, posted, transmitted or otherwise used in any form without the express written consent of the author.

Para Mamá y Papá con todo cariño y eterna gratitud

[*For Mom and Dad, with all my love and eternal gratitude*]

About the Author

http://www.victordlopez.com

Victor D. López is a tenured Professor of Legal Studies in Business at Hofstra University's Frank G. Zarb School of Business. He holds a Juris Doctor degree from St. John's University School of Law and a B.A. from Queens College, C.U.N.Y. (English Honors Program – Writing) and is a member of the New York State Bar, New York State Bar Association, the Academy of Legal Studies in Business (ALSB) and the North East Academy of Legal Studies in Business (NEALSB). He has been an academic for more than 25 years and, prior to joining the Hofstra University faculty, he served as a tenured Professor of Business, as Dean of Business and Business Information Technologies, and as Academic Dean in urban, suburban and rural public and private academic institutions.

He is the author of several textbooks and trade books and has written poetry and fiction throughout most of his life, some of which has been published in anthologies and literary magazines.

Previous Books by the Author

- *Business Law and the Legal Environment of Business 3e* (Textbook Media 2017)
- *Mindscapes: 10 Science Fiction and Speculative Fiction Short Stories* (Printed through CreateSpace, Kindle Direct and Smashwords, 2014. Audiobook version distributed by Audible and Amazon.)
- *Of Pain and Ecstasy: Collected Poems* (Printed by CreateSpace, Kindle Direct Publishing and CreateSpace, 2011)
- *Business Law: An Introduction 2e* (Textbook Media 2011)
- *Business Law and the Legal Environment of Business 2e* (Textbook Media 2010)
- *Free and Low Cost Software for the PC* (McFarland & Company 2000)
- *The Legal Environment of Business 1/e* (Prentice Hall 1997)
- *Case and Resource Materials for the Legal Environment of Business* (Prentice Hall 1997)
- *Business Law: An Introduction 1/e* (Irwin / McGraw Hill 1993)
- *Free and User-Supported Software for the IBM PC: A Resource Guide for Libraries and Individuals* (McFarland & Company 1990) (Co-authored with Kenneth J. Ansley)

[For a list of current published scholarly articles, you can visit http://www.hofstra.edu/faculty/fac_profiles.cfm?id=907 *or* http://www.victordlopez.com/recent-scholarly-articles.html]

A Note to My Readers

This book is intended as both a primer on copyright law and as a general reference for authors, artists, musicians, librarians, entrepreneurs and others interested in learning about the subject. The material in this book is largely excerpted from material that originally appeared in my earlier general reference book on intellectual property, *Intellectual Property Law: A Practical Guide to Copyrights, Patents, Trademarks and Trade Secrets* (© 2014, 2017). I've opted to release the material in an edited and expanded version as a stand-alone guide to copyright law for the benefit of individuals whose interest in intellectual property is limited to copyrights.

As you use this book, keep in mind that it can only offer general reference materials and information. While this book will provide you with timely, useful information and show you where you can find additional free resources through the U.S. Copyright Office, it does not offer legal advice. Only an attorney can provide you with legal advice tailored to your specific needs and neither this book nor any of the self-help advice offered by various national services that assist consumers with document preparation, including the creation and filing of patent, trademark and copyright applications, is a substitute for the advice of an experienced lawyer.

Acknowledgments

I am poor in all things save in the quality of my family and friends. The individuals to whom I have dedicated this book and my previous seven books have had an enormous influence in my life, as have others not yet unacknowledged. If able, I hope to correct that in the future. In case that opportunity is not open to me, I would at least like to express my gratitude for the privilege of the trans-formative nature of their friendship that time, distance and life can never change: Maria Luisa Seoane (Marisita), José Naveira (Tio Pepe), Maria Olga Naveira Calviño (Olguita), Francisco Naveira (Tio Paco), and Bill Raynor.

I would also like to acknowledge the support of Hofstra University's Frank G. Zarb School of Business of my research, publication and professional development efforts, including the summer research grants that facilitated the research, writing and publication of numerous scholarly articles over the past decade.

Finally, I need to acknowledge my colleagues and friends in the Department of Accounting, Taxation and Legal Studies in Business and throughout Hofstra University and the Frank G. Zarb School of Business, an extraordinary group of professionals with whom it is an honor and privilege to serve.

Table of Contents

Chapter 1: *1*

General Introduction to Copyright Law *1*

   Introduction 1

   Subject Matter of Copyright 2

   Exclusive Rights in Copyrighted Works 3

Chapter 2: *7*

Limitations on the Exclusive Rights of Copyright Owners *7*

   Fair Use Limitations of Exclusive Rights 7

      Reproduction by Libraries and Archives 9

Chapter 3: *12*

Copyright Ownership, Creation and Transfer *12*

   Copyright Ownership and Transfer 12

      The Difference Between Ownership of a Copyright and Ownership of Physical Objects 13

   Duration of Copyright 14

   A Cautionary Word About Works for Hire 15

   The Process of Securing a Copyright 16

Chapter 4: *19*

Copyright Registration *19*

   General Rules for Copyright Registration 19

   Application for Copyright Registration 20

Chapter 5: *23*

Remedies for Infringement and Criminal and Civil Sanctions *23*

   Civil Remedies for Infringement 23

   Criminal Penalties for Infringement 25

Chapter 6: *28*
Some Practical Considerations *28*
    Should Copyrighted Works be Registered? 28
    How Can I Tell if Something Is in the Public Domain? 29
    Fair Use of Copyrighted Works 30
    Copyright and Works of Art 32
Appendix A: *35*
Copyright Registration Forms *35*
Selected Sections of the Copyright Act of 1978 as Amended (Title 17 of the United States Code) *39*

Chapter 1:
General Introduction to Copyright Law

Introduction

The U.S. Constitution gives Congress the power "To promote the Progress of Science and useful Arts, by securing for limited Times to Authors and Inventors the exclusive Right to their respective Writings and Discoveries."[1] Congress exercised this right in passing the Copyright Act of 1790 which was signed into law by President George Washington on May 31, 1790. The Act was brief; it fit on a half-page of a newspaper.[2] It provided citizens of the United States copyright protection for the maps, charts, and books they authored for a period of 14 years and allowed copyright protection to be extended for an additional 14-year period. The Copyright Act has been amended numerous times in the intervening years and grown in both complexity and size. The current version of the Act[3] as of this writing is 266 pages not counting 12 appendices. Although the law has grown in complexity since the first Copyright Act, the core concepts relating to copyright are still relatively simple to understand. In this chapter, we will examine the essential elements of the law and the specific types of intellectual property it is intended to protect.

---

[1] U.S. Const. Art I §8.

[2] The Columbian Sentinel, July 17, 1790 at 1. A digitized version of the newspaper page can be viewed at
http://www.earlyamerica.com/earlyamerica/firsts/copyright/centinel.html
(last visited August 11, 2009).

[3] The current Act is contained in Title 17 of the U.S. Code and includes amendments through 2006.

Subject Matter of Copyright

The subject matter covered by the law of copyright is rather broad and includes "original works of authorship fixed in any tangible medium of expression, now known or later developed, from which they can be perceived, reproduced, or otherwise communicated, either directly or with the aid of a machine or device."[4] Works of authorship include the following categories:[5]

- literary works;
- musical works, including any accompanying words;
- dramatic works, including any accompanying music;
- pantomimes and choreographic works;
- pictorial, graphic, and sculptural works;
- motion pictures and other audiovisual works;
- sound recordings; and
- architectural works.

Copyright protection attaches to original works of authorship fixed in a permanent medium. Note that an original work of authorship is not protected as soon as it is created; rather protection attaches when it is fixed onto a permanent medium so that it can be reproduced and perceived by others at a later time. It is not the act of creation but rather the act of saving or archiving one's creation in a tangible medium that grants copyright protection to the creator. For example, if a poet constructs a new poem in her mind and speaks it aloud in a public place where others can hear it, no copyright attaches to this new creation. Copyright attaches only when the work is fixed in an existing or yet to be invented "tangible medium of expression" that allows it to be reproduced and perceived by others later. Writing the poem on paper with a pen or pencil will suffice, as would recording a reading of the poem on tape or in digital form saved as an audio or

---

[4] 17 U.S.C. §102(a) (2006).

[5] Id.

video file on a computer, compact disk, smartphone, DVD or some future medium of storage not yet in existence. Likewise, a new dance routine that is created by a choreographer is not copyrighted until it is "saved" in some form such as by being videotaped or by the choreographer writing down the steps in the dance on paper or some other permanent form through which the dance steps can later be communicated to and reproduced by others.

Thus, a photographer who snaps a photograph automatically obtains a copyright to it when the image is captured on film or saved in digital form to the camera's internal memory, or in an external SD card or other removable storage. And a writer's words are copyrighted as soon as they are transferred to paper by a pen or other writing implement or saved onto a computer's hard disk or removable storage (e.g., burned onto a CD or DVD or saved onto a USB thumb drive or other removable storage media).

Exclusive Rights in Copyrighted Works

The owner of a copyright has the exclusive right to do (and to authorize others to do) all of the following with regard to the work protected by the copyright:

(1) To reproduce the copyrighted work in copies or phonorecords

Only the copyright holder can make duplicates of copyrighted works in any medium that currently exists or is yet to be developed. If a poet writes a poem and saves it in a permanent form as previously described, only he can make copies of the poem, post it online, send it as an email attachment to friends and the like. And if he later records a reading of the poem, only he (or others with his permission) can distribute that recording.

(2) To prepare derivative works based upon the copyrighted work

Derivative works are new works based on an existing copyrighted work. For example, the movie Jaws is a derivative work of Herman Melville's classic novel Moby Dick. And West Side Story is a derivative work of Shakespeare's Romeo and Juliet. If the copyright to both original works had not expired long before the movies were made, both could be subjected to copyright infringement actions unless they were authorized by the respective authors. But once a copyright expires, the work becomes a part of the public domain and may be reproduced freely by anyone.

(3) To distribute copies or phonorecords of the copyrighted work to the public by sale or other transfer of ownership, or by rental, lease, or lending

Only copyright holders may reproduce their copyrighted audio works. Note that copyrighted material, be it of the print or audio variety, cannot be reproduced by anyone without the author's express consent regardless of whether it is distributed for a fee or free of charge.

(4) In the case of literary, musical, dramatic, and choreographic works, pantomimes, and motion pictures and other audiovisual works, to perform the copyrighted work publicly

Authors can control the public performance of their works. I can sing my favorite copyrighted tunes in the shower but cannot give a free public concert involving copyrighted music without appropriate permission and/or compensation of the copyright owners.

(5) In the case of literary, musical, dramatic, and choreographic works, pantomimes, and pictorial, graphic, or sculptural works, including the individual images of a motion picture or other audiovisual work, to display the copy-righted work publicly

You are free to set up a projection system in your media room and enjoy a recently released movie as it was intended to be seen but cannot show the movie to the public without permission or compensation of the copyright holder(s). But you can publicly project classic films whose copyrights have expired.

(6) In the case of sound recordings, to perform the copyrighted work publicly by means of a digital audio transmission.[6]

You can blast your stereo with your favorite tunes at home but cannot transmit these tunes by digital transmission publicly.

The exclusive nature of the enumerated rights means that no one other than the owner of a copyright (and those acting with his or her consent) may copy, distribute, publicly display, publicly perform or create derivative works based on the copyrighted work. Unauthorized use of copyrighted materials can lead to civil and criminal sanctions that will be discussed later in this chapter.

It is important to note that civil and criminal copyright infringement can occur even when unauthorized use of copyrighted work is made that does not bring any material benefit to the copyright infringer. Thus, while making unauthorized copies of a copyrighted book, music CD or of a video DVD for sale clearly involve both criminal and civil violations of copyright law, so does copying a rented movie to keep for personal use and/or to share with a friend, copying an audio book borrowed from the library, or burning a CD of one's favorite music to give to a friend.

By purchasing a legal copy of a copyrighted work such as a book, magazine, or legally downloaded MP3 music files, the user generally obtains the right to use those files for personal use only, and not to copy or redistribute them. Thus, you may watch a rented or purchased movie at home and show it to guests in your home for

---

[6] 17 U.S.C. §106 (2006).

non-commercial purposes (e.g., without charging them a fee). However, you cannot show the movie in a setting that is open to the public (e.g., on a projection system in your back yard where everyone is welcomed to view the movie).

The same is true for copyrighted work that is non-commercial in nature. The performance of an amateur rock band in someone's garage cannot be taped without the band's consent; and if consent is given to tape the performance, copies of the performance cannot be made without the express consent of the band, nor can the taped performance be posted online, broadcast or played at a public venue without the band's consent. And the same is true for a dance routine, short story, poem, drawing, painting, sculpture or any other subject matter protected by copyright.

Chapter 2:
Limitations on the Exclusive Rights of Copyright Owners

Fair Use Limitations of Exclusive Rights

The exclusive rights of a copyright owner are subject to some notable limitations. Chief among these is the fair use exception that allows limited use of copyrighted works for purposes of "criticism, comment, news reporting, teaching (including multiple copies for classroom use), scholarship, or research."[7] In determining whether a specific use of a copyrighted work constitutes fair use, the following criteria are evaluated:

(1) the purpose and character of the use, including whether such use is of a commercial nature or is for nonprofit educational purposes;

Greater latitude is given to nonprofit educational use, for example, than commercial use. This is not to say, however, that non-profit use permits extensive use of copyrighted material. It does not.

(2) the nature of the copyrighted work;

If, for example, the work is a photograph, it generally cannot be reproduced under fair use even for educational use or artistic criticism. On the other hand, quoting a few stanzas from a thousand-word poem is most probably covered by fair use as it will not reveal too much of the original work.

(3) the amount and substantiality of the portion used in relation to the copyrighted work as a whole;

---

[7] 17 U.S.C. §107 (2006).

Closely related to the last point, the longer the work the likelier that a reasonably small portion or it may be used for non-profit critical or educational purposes. Thus, quoting a page from a 300-page novel for purposes of a critical review or for classroom analysis is probably fine, but using a sonnet from a poetry book comprised of only six sonnets probably is not fair use.

(4) the effect of the use upon the potential market for or value of the copyrighted work.[8]

It is not merely the amount of material used as it relates to the whole that matters, but also the nature of that material. For example, if the page from the 300-page novel in the example under section 3 above gives away the book's surprise ending, it will never qualify as fair use since it will impact the ability of the author to sell the work once the surprise ending is disclosed.

In determining whether use of a copyrighted work constitutes allowable fair use, the courts will weigh the exclusive rights of copyright owners against the needs of academics and others to make reasonable use of copyrighted works for purposes of review, criticism, teaching and scholarship. Generally speaking, use of copyrighted materials for non-profit educational or scholarly purposes is more likely to be determined to be a fair use of the material than a similar use of material for commercial use. However, even when non-commercial use is involved, the amount of material used must be reasonable (e.g., a small fraction of the copyrighted work). Thus, as previously noted, quoting a paragraph from a novel in a book review would almost certainly be considered a fair use of the material, but not including an entire chapter of the novel in a book review. Likewise, showing a ten-second clip from a newly released movie without permission in a movie review is most likely a fair use

---

[8] *Id.*

of the material, but showing a ten-minute scene is not.

The courts also balance the potential impact of the material used on the value and market for the copyrighted work. Use of copyrighted material is likely to diminish its value or marketability for the copyright owner is less likely to be held to be a fair use of the material than a use that has no significant impact on the marketability of the work. Because fair use is a defense to a copyright infringement action that is weighed on a case-by-case basis by the courts, it is better to err on the side of caution and obtain permission to use copyrighted works even for non-commercial educational use rather than risk the potential of litigation and its uncertain outcome.

Reproduction by Libraries and Archives

A second important limitation on copyright owners' exclusive rights involves the reproduction of copyrighted works by libraries and archives. Section 108 of the Copyright Act[9] provides that it is not copyright infringement for libraries, archives or their employees in the regular course of their employment to reproduce one copy or phonorecord of a work if the following conditions are met:

(1) The reproduction or distribution is made without any purpose of direct or indirect commercial advantage;

(2) The collections of the library or archives are (i) open to the public, or (ii) available not only to researchers affiliated with the library or archives or with the institution of which it is a part, but also to other persons doing research in a specialized field; and

---

[9] 17 U.S.C. §108 (2006).

(3) The reproduction or distribution of the work includes a notice of copyright that appears on the copy or phonorecord that is reproduced under the provisions of this section, or includes a legend stating that the work may be protected by copyright if no such notice can be found on the copy or phonorecord that is reproduced under the provisions of this section.[10]

Libraries and archives may make up to three copies or phonorecords of an unpublished work duplicated solely for purposes of preservation and security or for deposit for research use in another library or archives provided that the copy or phonorecord reproduced is currently in the collections of the library or archives and that any such copy or phonorecord that is reproduced in digital format is not otherwise distributed in that format and is not made available to the public in that format outside the premises of the library or archives.[11]

Libraries and archives are also allowed to make up to three copies or phonorecords of a published work duplicated solely for the purpose of replacement of a copy or phonorecord that is damaged, deteriorating, lost, or stolen, or if the existing format in which the work is stored has become obsolete if the library or archives has, after a reasonable effort, determined that an unused replacement cannot be obtained at a fair price and as long as any such copy or phonorecord that is reproduced in digital format is not made available to the public in that format outside the premises of the library or archives in lawful possession of such copy.[12]

---

[10] 17 U.S.C. §108(a)(1)-(3) (2006).

[11] 17 U.S.C. §108(b)(1)-(2) (2006).

[12] 17 U.S.C. §108(c) (1)-(2) (2006).

The above exceptions allow libraries and archives to make legal reproductions of copyrighted works for purposes of preserving works or transferring works to a different medium when the medium in which they were originally acquired becomes obsolete and a copy of the work is not available at a reasonable price in a more accessible medium. For example, an audio book originally purchased on eight-track tape and no longer available at a reasonable price for purchase could be copied on to a cassette once eight-track tape and tape players become difficult to find. (If cassettes become obsolete in turn, it could then be copied onto a CD-ROM or other then-current medium of storage.) Once copied, the copy may be circulated *in place of* the original eight-track tape. This is not to say that multiple copies of the same work may be made and simultaneously circulated by the library or archive; that would, in fact, constitute copyright infringement.

Although individuals who make impermissible copies of copyrighted materials borrowed from a library are guilty of copyright infringement, libraries and archives will avoid liability for unsupervised infringement by users (e.g., by the use of photocopying machines or downloading and saving copyrighted material) provided that they post a notice by such equipment that the copy may be subject to copyright law.[13]

The rights of reproduction discussed here do not generally apply to a musical work, a pictorial, graphic or sculptural work, or a motion picture or other audiovisual work other than an audiovisual work dealing with news.[14]

---

[13] 17 U.S.C. §108(f)(1)-(2) (2006).

[14] 17 U.S.C. §108(i) (2006).

Chapter 3:

Copyright Ownership, Creation and Transfer

Copyright Ownership and Transfer

A copyright is a personal property right that vests in the author or authors of a work. In situations when a work is made for hire (e.g., when an author is contracted by a publisher to write a book in exchange for royalties and/or other payment), the copyright owner is the employer who commissions the work who owns all the rights provided in the copyright to the work absent a written agreement to the contrary.[15] In work for hire arrangements, the author may be credited with authorship of the work, but it is the employer who commissioned the work who owns the copyright and has the right to dispose of the work in any way it sees fit absent a contractual agreement to the contrary with the author.[16] The owner of a copyright may dispose of it the same as any other type of personal property. Namely, she may sell it, license it, or give it away during her life or after death by a provision in a valid will.

---

[15] 17 U.S.C. §201(b) (2006).

[16] This is the usual arrangement in the writing of college textbooks, for example. But a work for hire can result in work created by an employee in his role as employee, such as reports, artwork, web page designs, and other works of authorship produced by the employee in the normal course of employment that qualify for copyright protection. Absent an agreement to the contrary, including terms in an employment contract or in a collective bargaining agreement covering employees in a union environment, works of authorship produced on the job as part of an employee's work responsibilities generally belong to the employer.

The Difference Between Ownership of a Copyright and Ownership of Physical Objects[17]

When someone owns a copyright, she or he owns the right to the expression of an idea that has been put in a tangible form. The expression of that idea and the copyright are two distinct rights and transferring one does not automatically transfer the other. For example, if you purchased this book in paperback form, you own it and have the right to give it away, sell it to someone else or even destroy it. By purchasing a copy of this book, you did not purchase its copyright however. Thus, you may not copy the book to give away to someone else or post an electronic version of it online; such use would constitute copyright infringement and could subject you to both civil and criminal penalties.

The book is personal property, but the intellectual property—the copyright—is retained by the copyright owner. The same, of course, is true of movies, audio books and music distributed in traditional media such as compact disks and DVDs or downloaded electronically to be played on a computer or other electronic device. You own a copy of the movie or music that you purchase but can only use it in ways that do not infringe on the copyright owner's property rights. (E.g., you can give away the original DVD containing the latest new release after you view it, but you cannot make a copy of it to sell or give away to a friend.)

If you belong to a movie rental service that allow you to stream movies online, you may view the movie in accordance with your rental agreement either once or as many times as the agreement allows. But you may not copy the movie to your hard disk or burn it to a DVD or, for that matter, use screen capture software to save the movie or a video recorder to record if off your computer screen.

---

[17] See 17 U.S.C. §202 (2006).

Of course, you also may not hook up your computer to a video projection system and project the movie outdoors for your neighbors to enjoy. (Projecting the movie indoors for the benefit of non-paying guests, however, would be fine as long as the viewing is not open to the public.)

Duration of Copyright

Copyright in works created on or after January 1, 1978 last for the life of the author plus an additional 70 years after the author's death.[18] For works prepared by two or more authors, the copyright lasts for the life of the longest surviving author and for 70 years after the death of the longest surviving author.[19] Copyrights in works published anonymously or under a pseudonym will last for 95 years from the date of their first publication or 120 years from the date of creation, whichever expires first.[20] But if such works are registered prior to the expiration of this time period in the name or names of their true authors, then the copyright will extent to the usual life of the longest-lived author and 70 years after his or her death.[21]

In the case of works for hire, where an author is contracted to create material as an employee that is to be copyrighted by the employer (e.g., the publisher of college textbooks who owns the copyright to work created by its authors under the terms of the typical publication agreement), the copyright protection runs for 95 years from the date of first publication or 120 years from the date of creation, whichever

---

[18] 17 U.S.C. §302(a) (2006).

[19] 17 U.S.C. §302(b) (2006).

[20] 17 U.S.C. §302(c) (2006).

[21] *Id.*

expires first.[22]

Copyrights that became effective prior to January 1, 1978 generally lasted for 28 years from the date of creation, with an additional extension of 67 years available to authors, their heirs and to owners of copyrights that were commissioned as works for hire.[23]

A Cautionary Word About Works for Hire

For authors who agree to publish their work as a work for hire, it is imperative that they pay very close attention to the terms of the publishing contract. New authors eager to publish their book with a traditional publisher can be especially susceptible to signing disadvantageous contracts even when dealing with respected traditional publishing houses. Royalties and advances usually get close attention by prospective authors, but equally important (and, for me, critically important) issues are often ignored. Among these are such questions as what happens when the book goes out of print?

An author should always demand a clause in every contract for a transfer of copyright back to the author when the book is no longer published. Otherwise, the author will not be able to use her previous work as the basis of a revised or expanded edition with another publisher as she will not own the copyright to said work. It is also best to agree ahead of time if possible when a book will be considered "out of print". In the academic publishing market where books have a relatively short life without updates, a publisher can keep a book "in print" that is ten years old and that no one will adopt without active marketing efforts by part of the publisher and which prevents an author from updating and expanding the book and offering it to a competing publisher (or, for that matter, self-publishing the book or releasing it into the public domain).

---

[22] *Id.*

[23] 17 U.S.C. §304(a)(1)(A)-(C) (2006).

Most publishers will be unlikely to negotiate an objective means of determining when a book is out of print, but a publisher should not have any valid reason for refusing to include a reversionary right or transfer of copyright to the author on request once a book is no longer included in their catalog or actively marketed.

Another important factor to consider and negotiate in works for hire is a right of first refusal for authors to write subsequent editions of the book (when appropriate — critical for textbooks, for example) and any derivative works based on the book. A publisher could otherwise decide that your book was a good idea but that another author would be better to write an update (with the original author receiving nominal or no compensation for the subsequent work). The same is true if a publisher wants to license a customized version of the book. An author will not be able to prevent this in a work for hire situation but can at least negotiate the right of first refusal if a customized version of the book is licensed.

Even if an author is unable to negotiate the right of first refusal for subsequent editions or derivative works (e.g., different language versions, international versions with required changes to suit the target market, etc.), an author should always insist on being credited as the author or co-author of any such works. Otherwise it is possible to have derivative versions of one's work reproduced without appropriate authorship credit to the author of the original work.

The Process of Securing a Copyright

As previously noted, copyright protection attaches automatically to any work of authorship as soon as it is created and saved in a permanent form. It is not necessary to formally register the work with the U.S. Copyright Office for copyright protection to attach. However, and most importantly, copyright registration is a prerequisite to suing for copyright infringement. So that while copyright protection may attach automatically to a work of authorship fixed in tangible form, one may not begin a lawsuit to recover damages for infringement or to enjoin copyright infringement without registration.

The good news for authors, musicians, choreographers, actors, artists, architects, photographers, business people and all others who want to protect their works of authorship against infringement is that the process for registering one's copyright simple, quick, and can be accomplished at a very modest cost. Copyrighted material can be registered in the U.S. Copyright Office either by filing the required forms and payment through the mail or electronically. Of the two, the online method is less expensive and generally results in faster processing times.[24]

As of this writing, the filing fee for a registering a basic claim to a single work is $35 as long as it is not a work for hire and is the work of a single author.[25] The cost for other electronic filings is $55 and the registration cost is $85 if paper forms are filed through the mail.[26] The U.S. Copyright Office estimates that 90 percent of electronic filers will receive a copyright certificate within six months of filing a complete submission, while one-third will receive the certificate within

---

[24] The USCO provides tutorial assistance for using the electronic filing option at http://www.copyright.gov/register/index.html (last visited September 2, 2009).

[25] Information on all current filing fees and services can be found at https://www.copyright.gov/docs/fees.html. (last visited April 4, 2018). Information on current fees can also be obtained by telephone from the Copyright Public Information Office at (202) 707-3000, 8:30 a.m. to 5:00 p.m. eastern time, Monday through Friday, except federal holidays, and by writing the **Library of Congress, Copyright Office, 101 Independence Avenue, S.E., Washington, D.C. 20559-6000**.

[26] *Id.*

Ten weeks of filing.[27] Filings through the mail take a bit longer with 90 percent of certificates received within eight months of submission and one-third of filers receiving certificates within five months of filing.[28] (You will find links to the current forms in Appendix A.)

Copyright registration can generally be accomplished at any time when copyright protection is in force for both published and unpublished works. Whether registration is done electronically or by regular mail, a copy of the unpublished work o phonorecord must accompany the complete application along with the required fee.[29] If published work is involved, then two copies of the best edition of the published work or phonorecord must accompany the application.[30] If the copyright relates to an author's contribution to a published collected work (e.g., a chapter in a book or short story in a collection of short stories), a single copy of the published work or phonorecord must accompany the application.[31]

---

[27] http://www.copyright.gov/register/index.html (last visited September 6, 2009)

[28] *Id.*

[29] 17 U.S.C. §408(b)(1) (2006).

[30] 17 U.S.C. §408(b)(2) (2006).

[31] 17 U.S.C. §408(b)(3) (2006).

Chapter 4:
Copyright Registration

General Rules for Copyright Registration

Works protected by U.S. copyright law, whether registered or not, should carry a copyright notice. The notice is not technically required, as copyright attaches automatically when a covered work is created and saved in some permanent form (e.g., saved as an electronic file, printed or written on paper). However, having an appropriate copyright notice in the work prevents infringers from asserting the defense of innocent infringement to mitigate damages in an action for copyright infringement (e.g., that they reasonably thought the work was in the public domain or otherwise not protected by copyright). The notice should be in the form of the copyright symbol (the letter "C" enclosed in a circle: ©), the word "Copyright" or the abbreviation "Copr." followed by the year of first publication of the work and the owner's name (e.g., © 2018 Jane Doe, Copyright 2018 Jane Doe. or Copr. 2018 Jane Doe).[32] The copyright notice must be affixed in such a manner and location as to give reasonable notice of the claim of copyright.[33]

When sound recordings are involved, copyright notice includes a symbol of the letter P within a circle followed by the year of first publication of the sound recording and the author's name. (e.g., **(P)** 2010 Jane Doe)[34] The notice needs to be placed on the surface of the

---

[32] 17 U.S.C. §401(b)(1)-(3) (2006).

[33] 17 U.S.C. §401(c) (2006).

[34] 17 U.S.C. §402(b)(1)-(3) (2006).

phonorecord, or on the phonorecord label or container in such a way as to give reasonable notice of the claim or copyright.[35]

Application for Copyright Registration

Regardless of whether electronic filing or filing through the mail is used, the application for copyright registration must be filed in the appropriate form (See Appendix A) and must include all of the following information:

(1) [T]he name and address of the copyright claimant;

(2) In the case of a work other than an anonymous or pseudonymous work, the name and nationality or domicile of the author or authors, and, if one or more of the authors is dead, the dates of their deaths;

(3) If the work is anonymous or pseudonymous, the nationality or domicile of the author or authors;

(4) In the case of a work made for hire, a statement to this effect;

(5) If the copyright claimant is not the author, a brief statement of how the claimant obtained ownership of the copyright;

(6) The title of the work, together with any previous or alternative titles under which the work can be identified;

(7) The year in which creation of the work was completed;

(8) If the work has been published, the date and nation of its first publication;

---

[35] 17 U.S.C. §402(c) (2006).

(9) In the case of a compilation or derivative work, an identification of any preexisting work or works that it is based on or incorporates, and a brief, general statement of the additional material covered by the copyright claim being registered;

(10) In the case of a published work containing material of which copies are required by section 601 to be manufactured in the United States, the names of the persons or organizations who performed the processes specified by subsection (c) of section 601 with respect to that material, and the places where those processes were performed; and

(11) Any other information regarded by the Register of Copyrights as bearing upon the preparation or identification of the work or the existence, owner-ship, or duration of the copyright. If an application is submitted for the renewed and extended term provided for in section 304(a)(3)(A) and an original term registration has not been made, the Register may request information with respect to the existence, ownership, or duration of the copyright for the original term.[36]

If the required application forms, attachments and fees are complete, a certificate of registration under the seal of the Copyright Office will be issued once the Register of Copyrights determines the material submitted for registration meets the requirements for copyrightable subject matter. Otherwise, the Register of Copyrights will notify the registrant in writing of the reason for refusing to issue a certificate of registration (e.g., the material is not copyrightable, or the claim is invalid for any other reason).[37]

---

[36] 17 U.S.C. §409 (2006).

[37] 17 U.S.C. §410(a)(b) (2006).

If the certificate of registration is issued, the effective date of registration is the date when the complete registration application was received by the Copyright Office.[38]

---

[38] 17 U.S.C. §410(d) (2006).

Chapter 5:

Remedies for Infringement and Criminal and Civil Sanctions

Civil Remedies for Infringement

The Copyright Act provides a variety of remedies for copyright infringement and imposes both civil and criminal sanctions upon infringers.

The Act makes the equitable remedy of injunction available to copyright owners whose works are infringed. When copyright infringement occurs, the copyright owner can ask a court to issue a temporary or permanently injunctions (a court order requiring that an infringing activity cease). Because copyright involve federal law, the jurisdiction to hear such cases is reserved to the federal district courts and requests for injunctive relief as well as suits for damages can be brought in the federal district courts. Injunctive relief granted by any district court can be enforced everywhere in the United States.[39] In addition, courts can also order the impounding of infringing material and, upon a final judgment of infringement, its destruction or other final disposition.[40]

Plaintiffs in infringement actions may also sue either for actual damages or for statutory damages. If they elect to sue for actual damages, copyright owners are entitled to recover the actual damages suffered because of the infringement, and any profits of the infringer that are attributable to the infringement and are not taken

---

[39] 17 U.S.C. §502(b) (2006).

[40] 17 U.S.C. §503(a)-(b) (2006).

into account in computing the actual damages.[41] The copyright owner has the option of seeking statutory damages instead of actual damage (e.g., when actual damages are nominal or difficult to prove) at any time before the court enters a final judgment in the case. Statutory damages can be awarded at the court's discretion in any amount not less than $750 or more than $30,000 per infringement of any one work. Where more than one person is found guilty of copyright infringement, the liability is joint and severable[42] (e.g., the plaintiff can sue one or more of the co-infringers individually or as a group and recover the full amount of the judgment from any of the infringers. If one infringer is made to pay the entire amount, she or he can then sue the other co-infringers for reimbursement for their portion of the judgment.)

In cases where the copyright owner establishes and a court finds that the infringement was willful (e.g., carried out on purpose, with knowledge that the material improperly used was protected by copyright), a court may raise the judgment to up to $150,000.[43] On the other hand, if an infringer proves to the satisfaction of the court that he or she had no reason to believe that his or her acts constituted an infringement of copyright, then a court in its discretion can lower the statutory judgment to a sum of not less than $200.[44] Courts may also award court costs (except for cases involving infringement by the U.S. government or its employees) and reasonable attorney's fees to copyright owners at its discretion.[45]

---

[41] 17 U.S.C. §504(b) (2006).

[42] 17 U.S.C. §504(c)(1) (2006).

[43] 17 U.S.C. §504(c)(2) (2006).

[44] *Id.*

[45] 17 U.S.C. §505 (2006).

Criminal Penalties for Infringement

Willful copyright infringement is a criminal offense if it is made for purposes of commercial advantage or private gain if one or more copies or distribution of a copyrighted work or phonorecord is made.[46] The reproduction or distribution of copyrighted work or phonorecords with a total retail value of more than $1,000 within any 180-day period is also a criminal offense even if it is not done for the purpose of private gain or commercial advantage[47] (e.g., gratuitous copying or distributions of copyrighted materials including materials copied for personal use). Posting copyrighted material that is being prepared for commercial distribution but has not yet been commercially distributed on a public computer network is also a criminal offense if the person who posts the material knew or should have known that it was intended for commercial distribution.[48]

---

[46] 17 U.S.C. §506(a)(1)(A) (2006).

[47] 17 U.S.C. §506(a)(1)(B) (2006).

[48] 17 U.S.C. §506(a)(1)(C) (2006).

Distributions of 10 or more copies of phonorecords or one or more copy of a copyrighted work with a total retail value of $2,500 or more made for commercial gain can lead to a maximum sentence of 5 years in jail.[49] For second offenses, the maximum sentence is increased to not more than 10 years.[50] First offenses involving a total retail value of $2,500 or less carry a maximum sentence of one year.[51] In cases of infringement not made for commercial gain, the maximum penalty is three years of imprisonment if the retail value of the infringed work is at least $2,500 (six years in cases of second and subsequent offenses), or one year if the retail value of the infringed work is more than $1,000.[52] The posting of commercial material that is not yet commercially available but is intended for commercial distribution can carry a maximum penalty of five years (10 years for second and subsequent offenses) if it is done to gain commercial advantage or personal gain and three years (six years for second and subsequent offenses) if gratuitous infringement is involved.[53]

In addition to significant jail time for criminal infringement conviction, the Act provides a forfeiture provision that allows a court to order the destruction or other disposition of infringing copies or phonorecords and the implements, devices or equipment used in their creation.[54] Fraudulently inserting a false copyright notice on copyrighted material, knowingly distributing material with a false copyright notice, and fraudulently removing or altering a valid

---

[49] 18 U.S.C. §2319(b)(1) (2008).

[50] 18 U.S.C. §2319(b)(2) (2008).

[51] 18 U.S.C. §2319(b)(3) (2008).

[52] 18 U.S.C. §2319(c)(1)-(3) (2008).

[53] 18 U.S.C. §2319(d)(1)-(4) (2008).

[54] 17 U.S.C. §506(b) (2006).

copyright notice can all result in a fine not to exceed $2,500.[55] In a similar vein, making a material misrepresentation as to a material fact in an application for copyright registration is also punishable by a maximum fine not to exceed $2,500.[56] In addition, equipment used in the manufacturing, reproduction or assembling of infringing materials may be seized and forfeited to the U.S. government.[57]

The statute of limitations for bringing an action for criminal infringement is five years from the date that the cause of action arises.[58]

---

[55] 17 U.S.C. §506(c)-(d) (2006).

[56] 17 U.S.C. §506(e) (2006).

[57] 17 U.S.C. §509(a) (2006).

[58] 17 U.S.C. §507 (2006).

Chapter 6:

Some Practical Considerations

Should Copyrighted Works be Registered?

As discussed in Chapter 4, copyright attaches as soon as a work is created and saved in a permanent form. That being the case, is there really a need for registering a work with the U.S. patent and Copyright Office?

The answer depends upon your intended use of the copyrighted work and its potential marketability. If infringement occurs and there is an issue raised as to when copyright attached, having a registered copyright provides some independent evidence of the date of registration. The validity of a registered copyright can still be attacked by someone claiming prior copyright of the material, but absent independent, verifiable evidence of the date of creation or prior publication, registering one's copyright offers proof of the date of registration at least.

For example, if an author writes the great American novel but never publishes it and a copy of the manuscript is later discovered by an unscrupulous person that registers the copyright in his own name as author, the original author (or his estate if he is deceased) will need to prove both authorship and the prior copyright date of the work (e.g., that he wrote the novel and when it was first saved in a permanent form). That might be difficult to do for unpublished works.

A work can be registered at any time after its creation, but proof of registration with the U.S. Copyright Office is not conclusive proof of authorship or of the original date of the copyright which attaches not upon registration but upon the creation and saving in a permanent form of an original work.

Given the nominal fee for electronic registration of copyrights ($35 as of this writing), it pays to register copyrighted material as soon as practicable after its creation if it has potential marketable value. Litigation is expensive and time consuming and avoiding it is always preferable. On the other hand, registering every work one creates when it has no marketable value is not very useful and can be expensive for a budding author.

How Can I Tell if Something Is in the Public Domain?

Determining whether a work is in the public domain can be challenging. When a copyright expires, a work falls into the public domain and may be used by anyone for any purpose without permission. The same is generally true of materials that are prepared by the federal and state governments and their agencies. But things can get complicated in many circumstances. For example, court decisions and statutes that are created and published by state and federal sources are in the public domain. But annotated decisions published by the various court reporters and legal databases (e.g., Nexis and Lexis) are copyrighted. So are model acts such as the Uniform Commercial Code (UCC) created by the National Conference of Commissioners on Uniform State Laws (NCCUSL). So that if I want to include sections of the Uniform Commercial Code in an appendix for one of my textbooks, I need to get permission from the copyright holder (NCCUSL). But I don't need permission if I want to include the actual version of the UCC adopted in a specific state as that is in the public domain—as long as I don't use any annotations added by a publisher of the state code. Likewise, I am free to make, give away and sell copies of movies that are in the public domain because their copyright has expired. If I find an original black and white copy of *It's a Wonderful Life* or *Mr. Smith Goes to Washington* (two personal favorites of mine by my all-time favorite actor, Jimmy Stewart), I can copy it and post it online, burn it to DVDs and give away or sell these as I see fit. But the colorized versions of classic films (which I avoid in any case) are copyrighted by the companies which colorized them—until that copyright expires.

It is not always easy—especially for lay persons—to know when a particular work is in the public domain. And downloading copyrighted materials fraudulently or innocently mislabeled as public domain does not insulate one from an infringement action.

Fair Use of Copyrighted Works

As discussed in Chapter 2, the fair use exception allows portions of copyrighted work to be used as long as portions of the work used are very small in relation to the whole work and the use does not unreasonably affect the copyright holder's right to profit from the sale, leasing or other use of the copyrighted work. Some greater latitude is given for non-profit use such as for educational purposes or literary criticism than for commercial use. But "educational use" is not a license to copy or distribute copyrighted material.

If a professor wants to copy an article from The Wall Street Journal for use in her class, that is not a problem. Copying the entire front page of the paper, however, is a potential problem. Likewise, using one of the examples in any of my law-related textbooks for class discussion is perfectly fine. Copying a chapter from any of my textbooks to post online or distribute in class, however, is not fair use. Professors doing so would be liable for infringement, as would the institutions that they serve if they know or should know that this is happening (e.g., if a print shop is used to produce a "free textbook" for students containing one chapter from 13 different books, or if the material is made available on the university's computer). And even if I gave permission for such use, it would still be copyright infringement as my publisher would not give permission and I am the author of the textbooks but not the copyright holder while these are in print since all of my textbooks (and nearly all textbooks published through traditional publishers) are works for hire. Indeed, I would be guilty of copyright infringement if I scanned and posted copies of my own textbooks and made them accessible to my students free of charge for use in my own classes.

There are other fair use exceptions as well, including parody. Derivative works made from copyrighted works are deemed to be copyright infringement, but works intended to ridicule copyrighted works are not deemed to be infringing derivative works. Thus, *Space Balls*, a less than kind spoof of *Star Wars* by Mel Brooks does not infringe on *Star Wars*' copyright, because it makes fun of it. There is no bright line to distinguish parody from infringement, however. And when it comes to any "fair use" exception to copyright infringement one would do well to note that "fair use" is an affirmative defense to copyright infringement. Whether something is or is not fair use will need to be determined in a court of law AFTER someone is sued for infringement.

Given that defending oneself from a copyright infringement claim can be very expensive, it is little comfort to someone to know that if they are sued they will likely prevail as it can cost tens of thousands of dollars to determine whether something is or is not a parody, or whether too much material was used.

One can take comfort in the knowledge that fair use exists, but only to a point as in any but the most clear-cut instances when fair use may be applicable, someone acting in good faith may still end up having to go to court to "prove" that the infringement of copyright is, in fact, covered by the fair use exception. Given the cost and pervasiveness of litigation in the U.S., avoidance of the issue is almost always the preferable option.

Copyright and Works of Art

Individuals who hire writers, photographers and artists of all kinds to crate works for use in business should beware the distinction between purchasing art and owning a copyright in the artwork which are often two very separate things.

When art is commissioned, especially for use in or by businesses, it is critically important that the work either be clearly done as a "work for hire" in which case the artist is an employee creating work wholly owned (including its copyright) by the employer or at least having a properly drafted agreement that transfers both the artwork and its copyright to the owner. Else, one can buy artwork that the artist is free to reproduce and sell to others (e.g., prints, etc.) reducing the potential value and uniqueness of the artwork to the buyer.

Even worse, if artwork is purchased without a transfer of copyright, the artist retains the copyright and can prevent the buyer from copying, displaying publicly or posting photos of the artwork online. Imagine a scenario where a company pays tens of thousands of dollars for, say, a unique sculpture and, after it is delivered and placed in front of the corporate offices, is sued for copyright infringement if the company shows the sculpture in front of its building on any blog, stationary or company literature. Closer to home, imagine your wedding photographer sues you for copyright infringement if you scan and post a copy of your wedding photos on your web page or on a social media site.

Photographers own the copyright to their photographs. If you pay a photographer to photograph your corporate event but do not get either a copyright transfer as part of the agreement or at least the right to use the copyrighted photographs indefinitely for any purpose, including commercial purposes, the photographer can sue if any of these photographs are copied, reproduced, posted online or otherwise used without prior consent. And commissions of photography, graphic design, print matter, paintings, sculptures, written materials, videography or any other work subject to copyright protection are not generally considered "works for hire" unless the contract retaining the creator of the work specifically states it is a work for hire. Imagine paying a web site developed to build a website or having a web hosting service create a free web page for you, only to learn that you do not own the copyright to your own web pages and that you cannot port them to a different web hosting service if you choose to do so. Or imagine a graphic artist friend creating a novel image that you adopt as an identifying corporate logo for your new entrepreneurial venture. Further imagine that the business becomes highly successful and that your trademarked logo is closely identified with your successful company. Now imagine your (former) friend demanding $100,000 to transfer the copyright to you and threatening to sue to enjoin you from using as well as for copyright infringement if you don't pay up?

Copyrighted work that is produced by employees whose job it is to create such work automatically belongs to the employer. So that if a company hires a writer to create promotional material, the company owns the material automatically. Likewise, if a software company hires programmers to work on creating or improving software that the company uses or sells, the company owns the code that the programmers produce. But problems can arise when independent contractors are involved and the contract to retains their services is unclear as to who owns the copyrighted material they create, or what use such material can be put to when a work for hire or copyright transfer are not specified in the agreement.

Litigation in the United States is always expensive. And, unlike in almost all other countries around the world, individuals who are sued for alleged civil wrongs cannot recover all or even some of their attorneys' fees from the losing party if they prevail.[59] One exception is for willful copyright infringement for which a defendant found guilty of willful infringement can not only be subjected to criminal and civil penalties but can also be required to pay the attorneys' fees of the copyright holder.

When it comes to questions of fair use and works believed to be in the public domain, a good rule of thumb is "if in doubt, leave it out."

---

[59] See LEADING THE WORLD IN THE WRONG DIRECTION: IS IT TIME FOR THE UNITED STATES TO ADOPT THE WORLD STANDARD "LOSER PAYS" RULE IN CIVIL LITIGATION? Victor D. López and Eugene T. Maccarrone, N.E. Jnl. Of Legal Studies, Vol. 32, 1 (Fall 2014). Available online at http://www.nealsb.info/PDFs/vol32.pdf#page=9 (last visited April 7, 2018).

Appendix A:

Copyright Registration Forms[60]

 **Form TX**

Detach and read these instructions before completing this form.
Make sure all applicable spaces have been filled in before you return this form.

BASIC INFORMATION

When to Use This Form: Use Form TX for registration of published or unpublished nondramatic literary works, excluding periodicals or serial issues. This class includes a wide variety of works: fiction, nonfiction, poetry, textbooks, reference works, directories, catalogs, advertising copy, compilations of information, and computer programs. For periodicals and serials, use Form SE.

Deposit to Accompany Application: An application for copyright registration must be accompanied by a deposit consisting of copies or phonorecords representing the entire work for which registration is to be made. The following are the general deposit requirements as set forth in the statute:
  Unpublished Work: Deposit one complete copy (or phonorecord).
  Published Work: Deposit two complete copies (or one phonorecord) of the best edition.
  Work First Published Outside the United States: Deposit one complete copy (or phonorecord) of the first foreign edition.
  Contribution to a Collective Work: Deposit one complete copy (or phonorecord) of the best edition of the collective work.
  The Copyright Notice: Before March 1, 1989, the use of copyright notice was mandatory on all published works, and any work first published before that date should have carried a notice. For works first published on and after March 1, 1989, use of the copyright notice is optional. For more information about copyright notice, see Circular 3, *Copyright Notice*.

For Further Information: To speak to a Copyright Office staff member, call (202) 707-3000 or 1-877-476-0778 (toll free). Recorded information is available 24 hours a day. Order forms and other publications from the address in space 9 or call the Forms and Publications Hotline at (202) 707-9100. Access and download circulars, certain forms, and other information from the Copyright Office website at *www.copyright.gov*.

PRIVACY ACT ADVISORY STATEMENT Required by the Privacy Act of 1974 (P.L. 93-579)
The authority for requesting this information is title 17 U.S.C. §409 and §410. Furnishing the requested information is voluntary. But if the information is not furnished, it may be necessary to delay or refuse registration and you may not be entitled to certain relief, remedies, and benefits provided in chapters 4 and 5 of title 17 U.S.C.
The principal uses of the requested information are the establishment and maintenance of a public record and the examination of the application for compliance with the registration requirements of the copyright code.
Other routine uses include public inspection and copying, preparation of public indexes, preparation of public catalogs of copyright registrations, and preparation of search reports upon request.
NOTE: No other advisory statement will be given in connection with this application. Please keep this statement and refer to it if we communicate with you regarding this application.

LINE-BY-LINE INSTRUCTIONS

Please type or print using black ink. The form is used to produce the certificate.

 SPACE 1: Title

  Title of This Work: Every work submitted for copyright registration must be given a title to identify that particular work. If the copies or phonorecords of the work bear a title or an identifying phrase that could serve as a title, transcribe that wording *completely* and *exactly* on the application. Indexing of the registration and future identification of the work will depend on the information you give here.
  Previous or Alternative Titles: Complete this space if there are any additional titles for the work under which someone searching for the registration might be likely to look or under which a document pertaining to the work might be recorded.
  Publication as a Contribution: If the work being registered is a contribution to a periodical, serial, or collection, give the title of the contribution in the "Title of This Work" space. Then, in the line headed "Publication as a Contribution," give information about the collective work in which the contribution appeared.

 SPACE 2: Author(s)

  General Instructions: After reading these instructions, decide who are the "authors" of this work for copyright purposes. In the case of a "collective work," give the requested information about every "author" who contributed any appreciable amount of copyrightable matter to this version of the work. If you need further space, request Continuation Sheets. In the case of a collective work, such as an anthology, collection of essays, or encyclopedia, give information about the author of the collective work as a whole.
  Name of Author: The fullest form of the author's name should be given. Unless the work was "made for hire," the individual who actually created the work is its "author." In the case of a work made for hire, the statute provides that "the employer or other person for whom the work was prepared is considered the author."
  What Is a "Work Made for Hire"? A "work made for hire" is defined as (1) "a work prepared by an employee within the scope of his or her employment"; or (2) "a work specially ordered or commissioned for use as a contribution to a collective work, as a part of a motion picture or other audiovisual work, as a translation, as a supplementary work, as a compilation, as an instructional text, as a test, as answer material for a test, or as an atlas, if the parties expressly agree in a written instrument signed by them that the works shall be considered a work made for hire." If you have checked "Yes" to indicate that the work was "made for hire," you must give the full legal name of the employer (or other person for whom the work was prepared). You may also include the name of the employee along with the name of the employer (for example: "Elster Publishing Co., employer for hire of John Ferguson").
  "Anonymous" or "Pseudonymous" Work: An author's contribution to a work is "anonymous" if that author is not identified on the copies or phonorecords of the work. An author's contribution to a work is "pseudonymous" if that author is identified on the copies or phonorecords under a fictitious name. If the work is "anonymous" you may: (1) leave the line blank; or (2) state "anonymous" on the line; or (3) reveal the author's identity. If the work is "pseudonymous" you may: (1) leave the line blank; or (2) give the pseudonym and identify it as such (for example: "Huntley Haverstock, pseudonym"); or (3) reveal the author's name, making clear which is the real name and which is the pseudonym (for example, "Judith Barton, whose pseudonym is Madeline Elster"). However, the citizenship or domicile of the author *must* be given in all cases.
  Dates of Birth and Death: If the author is dead, the statute requires that the year of death be included in the application unless the work is anonymous or pseudonymous. The author's birth date is optional but is

---

[60] All copyright registration forms with instructions may be accessed at http://www.copyright.gov/forms/.

useful as a form of identification. Leave this space blank if the author's contribution was a "work made for hire."

Author's Nationality or Domicile: Give the country of which the author is a citizen or the country in which the author is domiciled. Nationality or domicile *must* be given in all cases.

Nature of Authorship: After the words "Nature of Authorship," give a brief general statement of the nature of this particular author's contribution to the work. Examples: "Entire text"; "Coauthor of entire text"; "Computer program"; "Editorial revisions"; "Compilation and English translation"; "New text."

SPACE 3: Creation and Publication

General Instructions: Do not confuse "creation" with "publication." Every application for copyright registration must state "the year in which creation of the work was completed." Give the date and nation of first publication only if the work has been published.

Creation: Under the statute, a work is "created" when it is fixed in a copy or phonorecord for the first time. Where a work has been prepared over a period of time, the part of the work existing in fixed form on a particular date constitutes the created work on that date. The date you give here should be the year in which the author completed the particular version for which registration is now being sought, even if other versions exist or if further changes or additions are planned.

Publication: The statute defines "publication" as "the distribution of copies or phonorecords of a work to the public by sale or other transfer of ownership, or by rental, lease, or lending." A work is also "published" if there has been an "offering to distribute copies or phonorecords to a group of persons for purposes of further distribution, public performance, or public display." Give the full date (month, day, year) when, and the country where, publication first occurred. If first publication took place simultaneously in the United States and other countries, it is sufficient to state "U.S.A."

SPACE 4: Claimant(s)

Name(s) and Address(es) of Copyright Claimant(s): Give the name(s) and address(es) of the copyright claimant(s) in this work even if the claimant is the same as the author. Copyright in a work belongs initially to the author of the work (including, in the case of a work made for hire, the employer or other person for whom the work was prepared). The copyright claimant is either the author of the work or a person or organization to whom the copyright initially belonging to the author has been transferred.

Transfer: The statute provides that, if the copyright claimant is not the author, the application for registration must contain "a brief statement of how the claimant obtained ownership of the copyright." If any copyright claimant named in space 4 is not an author named in space 2, give a brief statement explaining how the claimant(s) obtained ownership of the copyright. Examples: "By written contract"; "Transfer of all rights by author"; "Assignment"; "By will." Do not attach transfer documents or other attachments or riders.

SPACE 5: Previous Registration

General Instructions: The questions in space 5 are intended to show whether an earlier registration has been made for this work and, if so, whether there is any basis for a new registration. As a general rule, only one basic copyright registration can be made for the same version of a particular work.

Same Version: If this version is substantially the same as the work covered by a previous registration, a second registration is not generally possible unless: (1) the work has been registered in unpublished form and a second registration is now being sought to cover this first published edition; or (2) someone other than the author is identified as copyright claimant in the earlier registration, and the author is now seeking registration in his or her own name. If either of these two exceptions applies, check the appropriate box and give the earlier registration number and date. Otherwise, do not submit Form TX. Instead, write the Copyright Office for information about supplementary registration or recordation of transfers of copyright ownership.

Changed Version: If the work has been changed and you are now seeking registration to cover the additions or revisions, check the last box in space 5, give the earlier registration number and date, and complete both parts of space 6 in accordance with the instructions below.

Previous Registration Number and Date: If more than one previous registration has been made for the work, give the number and date of the latest registration.

SPACE 6: Derivative Work or Compilation

General Instructions: Complete space 6 if this work is a "changed version," "compilation," or "derivative work" and if it incorporates one or more earlier works that have already been published or registered for copyright or that have fallen into the public domain. A "compilation" is defined as "a work formed by the collection and assembling of preexisting materials or of data that are selected, coordinated, or arranged in such a way that the resulting work as a whole constitutes an original work of authorship." A "derivative work" is "a work based on one or more preexisting works." Examples of derivative works include translations, fictionalizations, abridgments, condensations, or "any other form in which a work may be recast, transformed, or adapted." Derivative works also include works "consisting of editorial revisions, annotations, or other modifications" if these changes, as a whole, represent an original work of authorship.

Preexisting Material (space 6a): For derivative works, complete this space *and* space 6b. In space 6a identify the preexisting work that has been recast, transformed, or adapted. The preexisting work may be material that has been previously published, previously registered, or that is in the public domain. An example of preexisting material might be: "Russian version of Goncharov's 'Oblomov.'"

Material Added to This Work (space 6b): Give a brief, general statement of the new material covered by the copyright claim for which registration is sought. *Derivative work* examples include: "Foreword, editing, critical annotations"; "Translation"; "Chapters 11–17." If the work is a *compilation*, describe both the compilation itself and the material that has been compiled. Example: "Compilation of certain 1917 speeches by Woodrow Wilson." A work may be both a derivative work and compilation, in which case a sample statement might be: "Compilation and additional new material."

SPACE 7, 8, 9: Fee, Correspondence, Certification, Return Address

Deposit Account: If you maintain a Deposit Account in the Copyright Office, identify it in space 7a. Otherwise leave the space blank and send the fee with your application and deposit.

Correspondence (space 7b): Give the name, address, area code, telephone number, fax number, and email address (if available) of the person to be consulted if correspondence about this application becomes necessary.

Certification (space 8): The application cannot be accepted unless it bears the date and the *handwritten signature* of the author or other copyright claimant, or of the owner of exclusive right(s), or of the duly authorized agent of author, claimant, or owner of exclusive right(s).

Address for Return of Certificate (space 9): The address box must be completed legibly because the certificate will be returned in a window envelope.

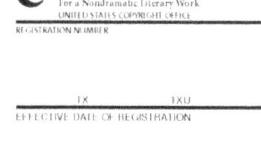

Form TX
For a Nondramatic Literary Work
UNITED STATES COPYRIGHT OFFICE

REGISTRATION NUMBER

TX TXU

EFFECTIVE DATE OF REGISTRATION

Month Day Year

Privacy Act Notice: Sections 408-410 of title 17 of the *United States Code* authorize the Copyright Office to collect the personally identifying information requested on this form in order to process the application for copyright registration. By providing this information you are agreeing to routine uses of the information that include publication to give legal notice of your copyright claim as required by 17 U.S.C. §705. It will appear in the Office's online catalog. If you do not provide the information requested, registration may be refused or delayed, and you may not be entitled to certain relief, remedies, and benefits under the copyright law.

DO NOT WRITE ABOVE THIS LINE. IF YOU NEED MORE SPACE, USE A SEPARATE CONTINUATION SHEET.

1

TITLE OF THIS WORK ▼

PREVIOUS OR ALTERNATIVE TITLES ▼

PUBLICATION AS A CONTRIBUTION If this work was published as a contribution to a periodical, serial, or collection, give information about the collective work in which the contribution appeared. **Title of Collective Work ▼**

If published in a periodical or serial give: **Volume ▼** **Number ▼** **Issue Date ▼** **On Pages ▼**

2 a

NAME OF AUTHOR ▼

DATES OF BIRTH AND DEATH
Year Born ▼ Year Died ▼

Was this contribution to the work a "work made for hire"? ❑ Yes ❑ No

AUTHOR'S NATIONALITY OR DOMICILE
Name of Country
OR { Citizen of ______ / Domiciled in ______

WAS THIS AUTHOR'S CONTRIBUTION TO THE WORK
Anonymous? ❑ Yes ❑ No
Pseudonymous? ❑ Yes ❑ No
If the answer to either of these questions is "Yes," see detailed instructions.

NATURE OF AUTHORSHIP Briefly describe nature of material created by this author in which copyright is claimed. ▼

NOTE

Under the law, the "author" of a "work made for hire" is generally the employer, not the employee (see instructions). For any part of this work that was "made for hire" check "Yes" in the space provided, give the employer (or other person for whom the work was prepared) as "Author" of that part, and leave the space for dates of birth and death blank.

b

NAME OF AUTHOR ▼

DATES OF BIRTH AND DEATH
Year Born ▼ Year Died ▼

Was this contribution to the work a "work made for hire"? ❑ Yes ❑ No

AUTHOR'S NATIONALITY OR DOMICILE
Name of Country
OR { Citizen of ______ / Domiciled in ______

WAS THIS AUTHOR'S CONTRIBUTION TO THE WORK
Anonymous? ❑ Yes ❑ No
Pseudonymous? ❑ Yes ❑ No
If the answer to either of these questions is "Yes," see detailed instructions.

NATURE OF AUTHORSHIP Briefly describe nature of material created by this author in which copyright is claimed. ▼

c

NAME OF AUTHOR ▼

DATES OF BIRTH AND DEATH
Year Born ▼ Year Died ▼

Was this contribution to the work a "work made for hire"? ❑ Yes ❑ No

AUTHOR'S NATIONALITY OR DOMICILE
Name of Country
OR { Citizen of ______ / Domiciled in ______

WAS THIS AUTHOR'S CONTRIBUTION TO THE WORK
Anonymous? ❑ Yes ❑ No
Pseudonymous? ❑ Yes ❑ No
If the answer to either of these questions is "Yes," see detailed instructions.

NATURE OF AUTHORSHIP Briefly describe nature of material created by this author in which copyright is claimed. ▼

3 a

YEAR IN WHICH CREATION OF THIS WORK WAS COMPLETED — This information must be given in all cases. ______ Year

b

DATE AND NATION OF FIRST PUBLICATION OF THIS PARTICULAR WORK — Complete this information ONLY if this work has been published. Month ______ Day ______ Year ______ Nation

4

COPYRIGHT CLAIMANT(S) Name and address must be given even if the claimant is the same as the author given in space 2. ▼

See instructions before completing this space.

TRANSFER If the claimant(s) named here in space 4 is (are) different from the author(s) named in space 2, give a brief statement of how the claimant(s) obtained ownership of the copyright. ▼

DO NOT WRITE HERE — OFFICE USE ONLY
APPLICATION RECEIVED
ONE DEPOSIT RECEIVED
TWO DEPOSITS RECEIVED
FUNDS RECEIVED

MORE ON BACK ▶ • Complete all applicable spaces (numbers 5-9) on the reverse side of this page. • See detailed instructions. • Sign the form at line 8.

DO NOT WRITE HERE
Page 1 of ______ pages

	EXAMINED BY		FORM TX
	CHECKED BY		
	☐ CORRESPONDENCE Yes		FOR COPYRIGHT OFFICE USE ONLY

DO NOT WRITE ABOVE THIS LINE. IF YOU NEED MORE SPACE, USE A SEPARATE CONTINUATION SHEET.

PREVIOUS REGISTRATION Has registration for this work, or for an earlier version of this work, already been made in the Copyright Office?
☐ Yes ☐ No If your answer is "Yes," why is another registration being sought? (Check appropriate box.) ▼
a. ☐ This is the first published edition of a work previously registered in unpublished form.
b. ☐ This is the first application submitted by this author as copyright claimant.
c. ☐ This is a changed version of the work, as shown by space 6 on this application.
If your answer is "Yes," give: **Previous Registration Number** ▶   **Year of Registration** ▶

5

DERIVATIVE WORK OR COMPILATION
Preexisting Material Identify any preexisting work or works that this work is based on or incorporates. ▼

a

6

See instructions before completing this space.

Material Added to This Work Give a brief, general statement of the material that has been added to this work and in which copyright is claimed. ▼

b

DEPOSIT ACCOUNT If the registration fee is to be charged to a deposit account established in the Copyright Office, give name and number of account.
Name ▼   **Account Number** ▼

a

7

CORRESPONDENCE Give name and address to which correspondence about this application should be sent. Name/ Address/ Apt/ City/ State/ Zip ▼

b

Area code and daytime telephone number ▶   Fax number ▶

Email ▶

CERTIFICATION* I, the undersigned, hereby certify that I am the
Check only one ▶
☐ author
☐ other copyright claimant
☐ owner of exclusive right(s)
☐ authorized agent of _____
of the work identified in this application and that the statements made   Name of author or other copyright claimant, or owner of exclusive right(s) ▲
by me in this application are correct to the best of my knowledge.

8

Typed or printed name and date ▼ If this application gives a date of publication in space 3, do not sign and submit it before that date.
_____ **Date** ▶ _____

Handwritten signature ▼

Certificate will be mailed in window envelope to this address:	Name ▼	**YOU MUST:** • Complete all necessary spaces • Sign your application in space 8
	Number/Street/Apt ▼	**SEND ALL 3 ELEMENTS IN THE SAME PACKAGE:** 1. Application form 2. Nonrefundable filing fee in check or money order payable to Register of Copyrights 3. Deposit material
	City/State/Zip ▼	**MAIL TO:** Library of Congress Copyright Office-TX 101 Independence Avenue SE Washington, DC 20559

9

*17 U.S.C. §506(e): Any person who knowingly makes a false representation of a material fact in the application for copyright registration provided for by section 409, or in any written statement filed in connection with the application, shall be fined not more than $2,500.

Form TX-Full Revised 07/2012 Printed on recycled paper   U.S. Government Printing Office: 2012-xxx-xxx/xx,xxx

Appendix B:
Selected Sections of the Copyright Act of 1978 as Amended (Title 17 of the United States Code)

§ 102 · Subject matter of copyright: In general

(a) Copyright protection subsists, in accordance with this title, in original works of authorship fixed in any tangible medium of expression, now known or later developed, from which they can be perceived, reproduced, or otherwise communicated, either directly or with the aid of a machine or device. Works of authorship include the following categories:

(1) literary works;

(2) musical works, including any accompanying words;

(3) dramatic works, including any accompanying music;

(4) pantomimes and choreographic works;

(5) pictorial, graphic, and sculptural works;

(6) motion pictures and other audiovisual works;

(7) sound recordings; and

(8) architectural works.

(b) In no case does copyright protection for an original work of authorship extend to any idea, procedure, process, system, method of operation, concept, principle, or discovery, regardless of the form in which it is described, explained, illustrated, or embodied in such work.

§ 105 · Subject matter of copyright: United States Government works

Copyright protection under this title is not available for any work of the United States Government, but the United States Government is not precluded from receiving and holding copyrights transferred to it by assignment, bequest, or otherwise.

§ 106 · Exclusive rights in copyrighted works

Subject to sections 107 through 122, the owner of copyright under this title has the exclusive rights to do and to authorize any of the following:

(1) to reproduce the copyrighted work in copies or phonorecords;

(2) to prepare derivative works based upon the copyrighted work;

(3) to distribute copies or phonorecords of the copyrighted work to the public by sale or other transfer of ownership, or by rental, lease, or lending;

(4) in the case of literary, musical, dramatic, and choreographic works, pantomimes, and motion pictures and other audiovisual works, to perform the copyrighted work publicly;

(5) in the case of literary, musical, dramatic, and choreographic works, pantomimes, and pictorial, graphic, or sculptural works, including the individual images of a motion picture or other audiovisual work, to display the copy-righted work publicly; and

(6) in the case of sound recordings, to perform the copyrighted work publicly by means of a digital audio transmission.

§ 107 · Limitations on exclusive rights: Fair use

Notwithstanding the provisions of sections 106 and 106A, the fair use of a copyrighted work, including such use by reproduction in copies or phonorecords or by any other means specified by that section, for purposes such as criticism, comment, news reporting, teaching (including multiple copies for classroom use), scholarship, or research, is not an infringement of copyright. In determining whether the use made of a work in any particular case is a fair use the factors to be considered shall include—

(1) the purpose and character of the use, including whether such use is of a commercial nature or is for nonprofit educational purposes;

(2) the nature of the copyrighted work;

(3) the amount and substantiality of the portion used in relation to the copy-righted work as a whole; and

(4) the effect of the use upon the potential market for or value of the copy-righted work.

The fact that a work is unpublished shall not itself bar a finding of fair use if such finding is made upon consideration of all the above factors.

§ 108 · Limitations on exclusive rights: Reproduction by libraries and archives

(a)Except as otherwise provided in this title and notwithstanding the provisions of section 106, it is not an infringement of copyright for a library or archives, or any of its employees acting within the scope of their employment, to reproduce no more than one copy or phonorecord of a work, except as provided in subsections (b) and (c), or to distribute such copy or phonorecord, under the conditions specified by this section, if —
(1) the reproduction or distribution is made without any purpose of direct or indirect commercial advantage;
(2) the collections of the library or archives are (i) open to the public, or (ii) available not only to researchers affiliated with the library or archives or with the institution of which it is a part, but also to other persons doing research in a specialized field; and
(3) the reproduction or distribution of the work includes a notice of copyright that appears on the copy or phonorecord that is reproduced under the provisions of this section, or includes a legend stating that the work may be protected by copyright if no such notice can be found on the copy or phonorecord that is reproduced under the provisions of this section.

(b) The rights of reproduction and distribution under this section apply to three copies or phonorecords of an unpublished work duplicated solely for purposes of preservation and security or for deposit for research use in another library or archives of the type described by clause (2) of subsection (a), if—

(1) the copy or phonorecord reproduced is currently in the collections of the library or archives; and

(2) any such copy or phonorecord that is reproduced in digital format is not otherwise distributed in that format and is not made available to the public in that format outside the premises of the library or archives.

(c) The right of reproduction under this section applies to three copies or phonorecords of a published work duplicated solely for the purpose of replacement of a copy or phonorecord that is damaged, deteriorating, lost, or stolen, or if the existing format in which the work is stored has become obsolete, if—

(1) the library or archives has, after a reasonable effort, determined that an unused replacement cannot be obtained at a fair price; and

(2) any such copy or phonorecord that is reproduced in digital format is not made available to the public in that format outside the premises of the library or archives in lawful possession of such copy.

For purposes of this subsection, a format shall be considered obsolete if the machine or device necessary to render perceptible a work stored in that format is no longer manufactured or is no longer reasonably available in the commercial marketplace.

(d) The rights of reproduction and distribution under this section apply to a copy, made from the collection of a library or archives where the user makes his or her request or from that of another library or archives, of no more than one article or other contribution to a copyrighted collection or periodical issue, or to a copy or phonorecord of a small part of any other copyrighted work, if—

(1) the copy or phonorecord becomes the property of the user, and the library or archives has had no notice that the copy or phonorecord would be used for any purpose other than private study, scholarship, or research; and

(2) the library or archives displays prominently, at the place where orders are accepted, and includes on its order form, a warning of copyright in accordance with requirements that the Register of Copyrights shall prescribe by regulation.

(e) The rights of reproduction and distribution under this section apply to the entire work, or to a substantial part of it, made from the collection of a library or archives where the user makes his or her request or from that of another library or archives, if the library or archives has first determined, on the basis of a reasonable investigation, that a copy or phonorecord of the copyrighted work cannot be obtained at a fair price, if—

(1) the copy or phonorecord becomes the property of the user, and the library or archives has had no notice that the copy or phonorecord would be used for any purpose other than private study, scholarship, or research; and

(2) the library or archives displays prominently, at the place where orders are accepted, and includes on its order form, a warning of copyright in accordance with requirements that the Register of Copyrights shall prescribe by regulation.

(f) Nothing in this section—

(1) shall be construed to impose liability for copyright infringement upon a library or archives or its employees for the unsupervised use of reproducing equipment located on its premises: *Provided*, that such equipment displays a notice that the making of a copy may be subject to the copyright law;

(2) excuses a person who uses such reproducing equipment or who requests a copy or phonorecord under subsection (d) from liability for copyright infringement for any such act, or for any later use of such copy or phonorecord, if it exceeds fair use as provided by section 107;

(3) shall be construed to limit the reproduction and distribution by lending of a limited number of copies and excerpts by a library or archives of an audiovisual news program, subject to clauses (1), (2), and (3) of subsection (a); or

(4) in any way affects the right of fair use as provided by section 107, or any contractual obligations assumed at any time by the library or archives when it obtained a copy or phonorecord of a work in its collections.

(g) The rights of reproduction and distribution under this section extend to the isolated and unrelated reproduction or distribution of a single copy or phonorecord of the same material on separate occasions, but do not extend to cases where the library or archives, or its employee—

(1) is aware or has substantial reason to believe that it is engaging in the related or concerted reproduction or distribution of multiple copies or phonorecords of the same material, whether made on one occasion or over a period of time, and whether intended for aggregate use by one or more individuals or for separate use by the individual members of a group; or
(2) engages in the systematic reproduction or distribution of single or multiple copies or phonorecords of material described in subsection (d): *Provided*, That nothing in this clause prevents a library or archives from participating in interlibrary arrangements that do not have, as their purpose or effect, that the library or archives receiving
such copies or phonorecords for distribution does so in such aggregate quantities as to substitute for a subscription to or purchase of such work.

(h)
(1) For purposes of this section, during the last 20 years of any term of copyright of a published work, a library or archives, including a nonprofit educational institution that functions as such, may reproduce, distribute, display, or perform in facsimile or digital form a copy or phonorecord of such work, or portions thereof, for purposes of preservation, scholarship, or research, if such library or archives has first determined, on the basis of a reasonable investigation, that none of the conditions set forth in subparagraphs (A), (B), and (C) of paragraph (2) apply.
(2) No reproduction, distribution, display, or performance is authorized under this subsection if—
(A) the work is subject to normal commercial exploitation;

(B) a copy or phonorecord of the work can be obtained at a reasonable price; or

(C) the copyright owner or its agent provides notice pursuant to regulations promulgated by the Register of Copyrights that either of the conditions set forth in subparagraphs (A) and (B) applies.

(3) The exemption provided in this subsection does not apply to any subsequent uses by users other than such library or archives.

(i) The rights of reproduction and distribution under this section do not apply to a musical work, a pictorial, graphic or sculptural work, or a motion picture or other audiovisual work other than an audiovisual work dealing with news, except that no such limitation shall apply with respect to rights granted by subsections (b), (c), and (h), or with respect to pictorial or graphic works published as illustrations, diagrams, or similar adjuncts to works of which copies are reproduced or distributed in accordance with subsections (d) and (e).

§ 201 · Ownership of copyright

(a) Initial Ownership. —Copyright in a work protected under this title vests initially in the author or authors of the work. The authors of a joint work are coowners of copyright in the work.

(b) Works Made for Hire. — In the case of a work made for hire, the employer or other person for whom the work was prepared is considered the author for purposes of this title, and, unless the parties have expressly agreed otherwise in a written instrument signed by them, owns all of the rights comprised in the copyright.

(c) Contributions to Collective Works. — Copyright in each separate contribution to a collective work is distinct from copyright in the collective work as a whole, and vests initially in the author of the contribution. In the absence of an express transfer of the copyright or of any rights under it, the owner of copyright in the collective work is presumed to have acquired only the privilege of reproducing and distributing the contribution as part of that particular collective work, any revision of that collective work, and any later collective work in the same series.

(d) Transfer of Ownership. —

(1) The ownership of a copyright may be transferred in whole or in part by any means of conveyance or by operation of law, and may be bequeathed by will or pass as personal property by the applicable laws of intestate succession.

(2) Any of the exclusive rights comprised in a copyright, including any subdivision of any of the rights specified by section 106, may be transferred as provided by clause (1) and owned separately. The owner of any particular exclusive right is entitled, to the extent of that right, to all of the protection and remedies accorded to the copyright owner by this title.

(e) Involuntary Transfer. — When an individual author's ownership of a copyright, or of any of the exclusive rights under a copyright, has not previously been transferred voluntarily by that individual author, no action by any govern-mental body or other official or organization purporting to seize, expropriate, transfer, or exercise rights of ownership with respect to the copyright, or any of the exclusive rights under a copyright, shall be given effect under this title, except as provided under title 11.2

§ 202 · Ownership of copyright as distinct from ownership of material object

Ownership of a copyright, or of any of the exclusive rights under a copyright, is distinct from ownership of any material object in which the work is embodied. Transfer of ownership of any material object, including the copy or phonorecord in which the work is first fixed, does not of itself convey any rights in the copy-righted work embodied in the object; nor, in the absence of an agreement, does transfer of ownership of a copyright or of any exclusive rights under a copyright convey property rights in any material object.

§ 302 · Duration of copyright: Works created on or after January 1, 1978

(a) In General. — Copyright in a work created on or after January 1, 1978, subsists from its creation and, except as provided by the following subsections, endures for a term consisting of the life of the author and 70 years after the author's death.

(b) Joint Works. — In the case of a joint work prepared by two or more authors who did not work for hire, the copyright endures for a term consisting of the life of the last surviving author and 70 years after such last surviving author's death.

(c) Anonymous Works, Pseudonymous Works, and Works Made for Hire. — In the case of an anonymous work, a pseudonymous work, or a work made for hire, the copyright endures for a term of 95 years from the year of its first publication, or a term of 120 years from the year of its creation, whichever expires first. If, before the end of such term, the identity of one or more of the authors of an anonymous or pseudonymous work is revealed in the records of a registration made for that work under subsections (a) or (d) of section 408, or in the records provided by this subsection, the copyright in the work endures for the term specified by subsection (a) or (b), based on the life of the author or authors whose identity has been revealed. Any person having an interest in the copyright in an anonymous or pseudonymous work may at any time record, in records to be maintained by the Copyright Office for that purpose, a statement identifying one or more authors of the work; the statement shall also identify the person filing it, the nature of that person's interest, the source of the information recorded, and the particular work affected, and shall comply in form and content with requirements that the Register of Copyrights shall prescribe by regulation.

(d) Records Relating to Death of Authors. — Any person having an interest in a copyright may at any time record in the Copyright Office a statement of the date of death of the author of the copyrighted work, or a statement that the author is still living on a particular date. The statement shall identify the person filing it, the nature of that person's interest, and the source of the information recorded, and shall comply in form and content with requirements that the Register of Copyrights shall prescribe by regulation. The Register shall maintain current records of information relating to the death of authors of copy-righted works, based on such recorded statements and, to the extent the Register considers practicable, on data contained in any of the records of the Copyright Office or in other reference sources.

(e) Presumption as to Author's Death. — After a period of 95 years from the year of first publication of a work, or a period of 120 years from the year of its creation, whichever expires first, any person who obtains from the Copyright Office a certified report that the records provided by subsection (d) disclose nothing to indicate that the author of the work is living, or died less than 70 years before, is entitled to the benefit of a presumption that the author has been dead for at least 70 years. Reliance in good faith upon this presumption shall be a complete defense to any action for infringement under this title.

§ 303 · Duration of copyright: Works created but not published or copyrighted before January 1, 1978

(a) Copyright in a work created before January 1, 1978, but not theretofore in the public domain or copyrighted, subsists from January 1, 1978, and endures for the term provided by section 302. In no case, however, shall the term of copyright in such a work expire before December 31, 2002; and, if the work is published on or before December 31, 2002, the term of copyright shall not expire before December 31, 2047.

(b) The distribution before January 1, 1978, of a phonorecord shall not for any purpose constitute a publication of the musical work embodied therein.

§ 304 · Duration of copyright: Subsisting copyrights

(a) COPYRIGHTS IN THEIR FIRST TERM ON JANUARY 1, 1978.—
(1)(A) Any copyright, the first term of which is subsisting on January 1, 1978, shall endure for 28 years from the date it was originally secured.

(B) In the case of—
(i) any posthumous work or of any periodical, cyclopedic, or other composite work upon which the copyright was originally secured by the proprietor thereof, or
(ii) any work copyrighted by a corporate body (otherwise than as assignee or licensee of the individual author) or by an employer for whom such work is made for hire,
the proprietor of such copyright shall be entitled to a renewal and extension of the copyright in such work for the further term of 67 years.

(C) In the case of any other copyrighted work, including a contribution by an individual author to a periodical or to a cyclopedic or other composite work—

(i) the author of such work, if the author is still living,
(ii) the widow, widower, or children of the author, if the author is not living,
(iii) the author's executors, if such author, widow, widower, or children are not living, or
(iv) the author's next of kin, in the absence of a will of the author,
shall be entitled to a renewal and extension of the copyright in such work for a further term of 67 years.

(2)(A) At the expiration of the original term of copyright in a work specified in paragraph (1)(B) of this subsection, the copyright shall endure for a renewed and extended further term of 67 years, which—
(i) if an application to register a claim to such further term has been made to the Copyright Office within 1 year before the expiration of the original term of copyright, and the claim is registered, shall vest, upon the beginning of such further term, in the proprietor of the copyright who is entitled to claim the renewal of copyright at the time the application is made; or
(ii) if no such application is made or the claim pursuant to such application is not registered, shall vest, upon the beginning of such further term, in the person or entity that was the proprietor of the copyright as of the last day of the original term of copyright.

(B) At the expiration of the original term of copyright in a work specified in paragraph (1)(C) of this subsection, the copyright shall endure for a renewed and extended further term of 67 years, which—

(i) if an application to register a claim to such further term has been made to the Copyright Office within 1 year before the expiration of the original term of copyright, and the claim is registered, shall vest, upon the beginning of such further term, in any person who is entitled under paragraph (1)(C) to the renewal and extension of the copyright at the time the application is made; or

(ii) if no such application is made or the claim pursuant to such application is not registered, shall vest, upon the beginning of such further term, in any person entitled under paragraph (1)(C), as of the last day of the original term of copyright, to the renewal and extension of the copyright.

(3) (A) An application to register a claim to the renewed and extended term of copyright in a work may be made to the Copyright Office—

(i) within 1 year before the expiration of the original term of copyright by any person entitled under paragraph (1)(B) or (C) to such further term of 67 years; and

(ii) at any time during the renewed and extended term by any person in whom such further term vested, under paragraph (2)(A) or (B), or by any successor or assign of such person, if the application is made in the name of such person.

(B) Such an application is not a condition of the renewal and extension of the copyright in a work for a further term of 67 years.

(4)(A) If an application to register a claim to the renewed and extended term of copyright in a work is not made within 1 year before the expiration of the original term of copyright in a work, or if the claim pursuant to such application is not registered, then a derivative work prepared under authority of a grant of a transfer or license of the copyright that is made before the expiration of the original term of copyright may continue to be used under the terms of the grant during the renewed and extended term of copyright without infringing the copyright, except that such use does not extend to the preparation during such renewed and extended term of other derivative works based upon the copyrighted work covered by such grant.

(B) If an application to register a claim to the renewed and extended term of copyright in a work is made within 1 year before its expiration, and the claim is registered, the certificate of such registration shall constitute prima facie evidence as to the validity of the copyright during its renewed and extended term and of the facts stated in the certificate. The evidentiary weight to be accorded the certificates of a registration of a renewed and extended term of copyright made after the end of that 1-year period shall be within the discretion of the court.

(b) COPYRIGHTS IN THEIR RENEWAL TERM AT THE TIME OF THE EFFECTIVE DATE OF THE SONNY BONO COPYRIGHT TERM EXTENSION ACT.—
Any copyright still in its renewal term at the time that the Sonny Bono Copyright Term Extension Act becomes effective shall have a copyright term of 95 years from the date copyright was originally secured.

(c) TERMINATION OF TRANSFERS AND LICENSES COVERING EXTENDED RENEWAL TERM. — In the case of any copyright subsisting in either its first or renewal term on January 1, 1978, other than a copyright in a work made for hire, the exclusive or nonexclusive grant of a transfer or license of the renewal copyright or any right under it, executed before January 1, 1978, by any of the persons designated by subsection (a)(1)(C) of this section, otherwise than by will, is subject to termination under the following conditions:

(1) In the case of a grant executed by a person or persons other than the author, termination of the grant may be effected by the surviving person or persons who executed it. In the case of a grant executed by one or more of the authors of the work, termination of the grant may be effected, to the extent of a particular author's share in the ownership of the renewal copyright, by the author who executed it or, if such author is dead, by the person or persons who, under clause (2) of this subsection, own and are entitled to exercise a total of more than one-half of that author's termination interest.

(2) Where an author is dead, his or her termination interest is owned, and may be exercised, as follows:

(A) The widow or widower owns the author's entire termination interest unless there are any surviving children or grandchildren of the author, in which case the widow or widower owns one-half of the author's interest.

(B) The author's surviving children, and the surviving children of any dead child of the author, own the author's entire termination interest unless there is a widow or widower, in which case the ownership of one-half of the author's interest is divided among them.

(C) The rights of the author's children and grandchildren are in all cases divided among them and exercised on a per stirpes basis according to the number of such author's children represented; the share of the children of a dead child in a termination interest can be exercised only by the action of a majority of them.

(D) In the event that the author's widow or widower, children, and grandchildren are not living, the author's executor, administrator, personal representative, or trustee shall own the author's entire termination interest.

(3) Termination of the grant may be effected at any time during a period of five years beginning at the end of fifty-six years from the date copyright was originally secured, or beginning on January 1, 1978, whichever is later.

(4) The termination shall be effected by serving an advance notice in writing upon the grantee or the grantee's successor in title. In the case of a grant executed by a person or persons other than the author, the notice shall be signed by all of those entitled to terminate the grant under clause (1) of this subsection, or by their duly authorized agents. In the case of a grant executed by one or more of the authors of the work, the notice as to any one author's share shall be signed by that author or his or her duly authorized agent or, if that author is dead, by the number and proportion of the owners of his or her termination interest required under clauses (1) and (2) of this subsection, or by their duly authorized agents.

(A) The notice shall state the effective date of the termination, which shall fall within the five-year period specified by clause (3) of this subsection, or, in the case of a termination under subsection (d), within the five-year period specified by subsection (d)(2), and the notice shall be served not less than two or more than ten years before that date. A copy of the notice shall be recorded in the Copyright Office before the effective date of termination, as a condition to its taking effect.

(B) The notice shall comply, in form, content, and manner of service, with requirements that the Register of Copyrights shall prescribe by regulation.

(5) Termination of the grant may be effected notwithstanding any agreement to the contrary, including an agreement to make a will or to make any future grant.

(6) In the case of a grant executed by a person or persons other than the author, all rights under this title that were covered by the terminated grant revert, upon the effective date of termination, to all of those entitled to terminate the grant under clause (1) of this subsection. In the case of a grant executed by one or more of the authors of the work, all of a particular author's rights under this title that were covered by the terminated grant revert, upon the effective date of termination, to that author or, if that author is dead, to the persons owning his or her termination interest under clause (2) of this subsection, including those owners who did not join in signing the notice of termination under clause (4) of this subsection. In all cases the reversion of rights is subject to the following limitations:

(A) A derivative work prepared under authority of the grant before its termination may continue to be utilized under the terms of the grant after its termination, but this privilege does not extend to the preparation after the termination of other derivative works based upon the copyrighted work covered by the terminated grant.

(B) The future rights that will revert upon termination of the grant become vested on the date the notice of termination has been served as provided by clause (4) of this subsection.

(C) Where the author's rights revert to two or more persons under clause (2) of this subsection, they shall vest in those persons in the proportionate shares provided by that clause. In such a case, and subject to the provisions of subclause (D) of this clause, a further grant, or agreement to make a further grant, of a particular author's share with respect to any right covered by a terminated grant is valid only if it is signed by the same number and proportion of the owners, in whom the right has vested under this clause, as are required to terminate the grant under clause (2) of this subsection. Such further grant or agreement is effective with respect to all of the persons in whom the right it covers has vested under this subclause, including those who did not join in signing it. If any person dies after rights under a terminated grant have vested in him or her, that person's legal representatives, legatees, or heirs at law represent him or her for purposes of this subclause.

(D) A further grant, or agreement to make a further grant, of any right covered by a terminated grant is valid only if it is made after the effective date of the termination. As an exception, however, an agreement for such a further grant may be made between the author or any of the persons provided by the first sentence of clause (6) of this subsection, or between the persons provided by subclause (C) of this clause, and the original grantee or such grantee's successor in title, after the notice of termination has been served as provided by clause (4) of this subsection.

(E) Termination of a grant under this subsection affects only those rights covered by the grant that arise under this title, and in no way affects rights arising under any other Federal State, or foreign laws.

(F) Unless and until termination is effected under this subsection, the grant, if it does not provide otherwise, continues in effect for the remainder of the extended renewal term.

(d) TERMINATION RIGHTS PROVIDED IN SUBSECTION (C) WHICH HAVE EXPIRED ON OR BEFORE THE EFFECTIVE DATE OF THE SONNY BONO COPYRIGHT TERM EXTENSION ACT. — In the case of any copyright other than a work made for hire, subsisting in its renewal term on the effective date of the Sonny Bono Copyright Term Extension Act for which the termination right provided in subsection (c) has expired by such date, where the author or owner of the termination right has not previously exercised such termination right, the exclusive or nonexclusive grant of a transfer or license of the renewal copyright or any right under it, executed before January 1, 1978, by any of the persons designated in subsection (a)(1)(C) of this section, other than by will, is subject to termination under the following conditions:

(1) The conditions specified in subsections (c)(1), (2), (4), (5), and (6) of this section apply to terminations of the last 20 years of copyright term as provided by the amendments made by the Sonny Bono Copyright Term Extension Act.

(2) Termination of the grant may be effected at any time during a period of 5 years beginning at the end of 75 years from the date copyright was originally secured.

§ 401. Notice of copyright: Visually perceptible copies

(a) General Provisions. — Whenever a work protected under this title is published in the United States or elsewhere by authority of the copyright owner, a notice of copyright as provided by this section may be placed on publicly distributed copies from which the work can be visually perceived, either directly or with the aid of a machine or device.

(b) Form of Notice. — If a notice appears on the copies, it shall consist of the following three elements:

(1) the symbol © (the letter C in a circle), or the word "Copyright", or the abbreviation "Copr."; and

(2) the year of first publication of the work; in the case of compilations or derivative works incorporating previously published material, the year date of first publication of the compilation or derivative work is sufficient. The year date may be omitted where a pictorial, graphic, or sculptural work, with accompanying text matter, if any, is reproduced in or on greeting cards, postcards, stationery, jewelry, dolls, toys, or any useful articles; and

(3) the name of the owner of copyright in the work, or an abbreviation by which the name can be recognized, or a generally known alternative designation of the owner.

(c) Position of Notice. — The notice shall be affixed to the copies in such manner and location as to give reasonable notice of the claim of copyright. The Register of Copyrights shall prescribe by regulation, as examples, specific methods of affixation and positions of the notice on various types of works that will satisfy this requirement, but these specifications shall not be considered exhaustive.

(d) Evidentiary Weight of Notice. — If a notice of copyright in the form and position specified by this section appears on the published copy or copies to which a defendant in a copyright infringement suit had access, then no weight shall be given to such a defendant's interposition of a defense based on innocent infringement in mitigation of actual or statutory damages, except as provided in the last sentence of section 504(c)(2).

§ 402. Notice of copyright: Phonorecords of sound recordings

(a) General Provisions. — Whenever a sound recording protected under this title is published in the United States or elsewhere by authority of the copyright owner, a notice of copyright as provided by this section may be placed on publicly distributed phonorecords of the sound recording.

(b) Form of Notice. — If a notice appears on the phonorecords, it shall consist of the following three elements:

(1) the symbol (P) (the letter P in a circle); and

(2) the year of first publication of the sound recording; and

(3) the name of the owner of copyright in the sound recording, or an abbreviation by which the name can be recognized, or a generally known alternative designation of the owner; if the producer of the sound recording is named on the phonorecord labels or containers, and if no other name appears in conjunction with the notice, the producer's name shall be considered a part of the notice.

(c) Position of Notice. — The notice shall be placed on the surface of the phonorecord, or on the phonorecord label or container, in such manner and location as to give reasonable notice of the claim of copyright.

(d) Evidentiary Weight of Notice. — If a notice of copyright in the form and position specified by this section appears on the published phonorecord or phonorecords to which a defendant in a copyright infringement suit had access, then no weight shall be given to such a defendant's interposition of a defense based on innocent infringement in mitigation of actual or statutory damages, except as provided in the last sentence of section 504(c)(2).

§ 403. Notice of copyright: Publications incorporating United States Government works

Sections 401(d) and 402(d) shall not apply to a work published in copies or phonorecords consisting predominantly of one or more works of the United States Government unless the notice of copyright appearing on the published copies or phonorecords to which a defendant in the copyright infringement suit had access includes a statement identifying, either affirmatively or negatively, those portions of the copies or phonorecords embodying any work or works protected under this title.

§ 404. Notice of copyright: Contributions to collective works

(a) A separate contribution to a collective work may bear its own notice of copyright, as provided by sections 401 through 403. However, a single notice applicable to the collective work as a whole is sufficient to invoke the provisions of section 401(d) or 402(d), as applicable with respect to the separate contributions it contains (not including advertisements inserted on behalf of persons other than the owner of copyright in the collective work), regardless of the ownership of copyright in the contributions and whether or not they have been previously published.

(b) With respect to copies and phonorecords publicly distributed by authority of the copyright owner before the effective date of the Berne Convention Implementation Act of 1988, where the person named in a single notice applicable to a collective work as a whole is not the owner of copyright in a separate contribution that does not bear its own notice, the case is governed by the provisions of section 406(a).

§ 405. Notice of copyright: Omission of notice on certain copies and phonorecords[5]

(a) Effect of Omission on Copyright. — With respect to copies and phonorecords publicly distributed by authority of the copyright owner before the effective date of the Berne Convention Implementation Act of 1988, the omission of the copyright notice described in sections 401 through 403 from copies or phonorecords publicly distributed by authority of the copyright owner does not invalidate the copyright in a work if —

(1) the notice has been omitted from no more than a relatively small number of copies or phonorecords distributed to the public; or

(2) registration for the work has been made before or is made within five years after the publication without notice, and a reasonable effort is made to add notice to all copies or phonorecords that are distributed to the public in the United States after the omission has been discovered; or

(3) the notice has been omitted in violation of an express requirement in writing that, as a condition of the copyright owner's authorization of the public distribution of copies or phonorecords, they bear the prescribed notice.

(b) Effect of Omission on Innocent Infringers. — Any person who innocently infringes a copyright, in reliance upon an authorized copy or phonorecord from which the copyright notice has been omitted and which was publicly distributed by authority of the copyright owner before the effective date of the Berne Convention Implementation Act of 1988, incurs no liability for actual or statutory damages under section 504 for any infringing acts committed before receiving actual notice that registration for the work has been made under section 408, if such person proves that he or she was misled by the omission of notice. In a suit for infringement in such a case the court may allow or disallow recovery of any of the infringer's profits attributable to the infringement, and may enjoin the continuation of the infringing undertaking or may require, as a condition for permitting the continuation of the infringing undertaking, that the infringer pay the copyright owner a reasonable license fee in an amount and on terms fixed by the court.

(c) Removal of Notice. — Protection under this title is not affected by the removal, destruction, or obliteration of the notice, without the authorization of the copyright owner, from any publicly distributed copies or phonorecords.

§ 406. Notice of copyright: Error in name or date on certain copies and phonorecords[6]

(a) Error in Name. — With respect to copies and phonorecords publicly distributed by authority of the copyright owner before the effective date of the Berne Convention Implementation Act of 1988, where the person named in the copyright notice on copies or phonorecords publicly distributed by authority of the copyright owner is not the owner of copyright, the validity and ownership of the copyright are not affected. In such a case, however, any person who innocently begins an undertaking that infringes the copyright has a complete defense to any action for such infringement if such person proves that he or she was misled by the notice and began the undertaking in good faith under a purported transfer or license from the person named therein, unless before the undertaking was begun-

(1) registration for the work had been made in the name of the owner of copyright; or

(2) a document executed by the person named in the notice and showing the ownership of the copyright had been recorded.

The person named in the notice is liable to account to the copyright owner for all receipts from transfers or licenses purportedly made under the copyright by the person named in the notice.

(b) Error in Date. — When the year date in the notice on copies or phonorecords distributed before the effective date of the Berne Convention Implementation Act of 1988 by authority of the copyright owner is earlier than the year in which publication first occurred, any period computed from the year of first publication under section 302 is to be computed from the year in the notice. Where the year date is more than one year later than the year in which publication first occurred, the work is considered to have been published without any notice and is governed by the provisions of section 405.

(c) Omission of Name or Date. — Where copies or phonorecords publicly distributed before the effective date of the Berne Convention Implementation Act of 1988 by authority of the copyright owner contain no name or no date that could reasonably be considered a part of the notice, the work is considered to have been published without any notice and is governed by the provisions of section 405 as in effect on the day before the effective date of the Berne Convention Implementation Act of 1988.

§ 407. Deposit of copies or phonorecords for Library of Congress

(a) Except as provided by subsection (c), and subject to the provisions of subsection (e), the owner of copyright or of the exclusive right of publication in a work published in the United States shall deposit, within three months after the date of such publication —

(1) two complete copies of the best edition; or

(2) if the work is a sound recording, two complete phonorecords of the best edition, together with any printed or other visually perceptible material published with such phonorecords.

Neither the deposit requirements of this subsection nor the acquisition provisions of subsection (e) are conditions of copyright protection.

(b) The required copies or phonorecords shall be deposited in the Copyright Office for the use or disposition of the Library of Congress. The Register of Copyrights shall, when requested by the depositor and upon payment of the fee prescribed by section 708, issue a receipt for the deposit.

(c) The Register of Copyrights may by regulation exempt any categories of material from the deposit requirements of this section, or require deposit of only one copy or phonorecord with respect to any categories. Such regulations shall provide either for complete exemption from the deposit requirements of this section, or for alternative forms of deposit aimed at providing a satisfactory archival record of a work without imposing practical or financial hardships on the depositor, where the individual author is the owner of copyright in a pictorial, graphic, or sculptural work and (i) less than five copies of the work have been published, or (ii) the work has been published in a limited edition consisting of numbered copies, the monetary value of which would make the mandatory deposit of two copies of the best edition of the work burdensome, unfair, or unreasonable.

(d) At any time after publication of a work as provided by subsection(a), the Register of Copyrights may make written demand for the required deposit on any of the persons obligated to make the deposit under subsection (a). Unless deposit is made within three months after the demand is received, the person or persons on whom the demand was made are liable —

(1) to a fine of not more than $250 for each work; and

(2) to pay into a specially designated fund in the Library of Congress the total retail price of the copies or phonorecords demanded, or, if no retail price has been fixed, the reasonable cost to the Library of Congress of acquiring them; and

(3) to pay a fine of $2,500, in addition to any fine or liability imposed under clauses (1) and (2), if such person willfully or repeatedly fails or refuses to comply with such a demand.

(e) With respect to transmission programs that have been fixed and transmitted to the public in the United States but have not been published, the Register of Copyrights shall, after consulting with the Librarian of Congress and other interested organizations and officials, establish regulations governing the acquisition, through deposit or otherwise, of copies or phonorecords of such programs for the collections of the Library of Congress.

(1) The Librarian of Congress shall be permitted, under the standards and conditions set forth in such regulations, to make a fixation of a transmission program directly from a transmission to the public, and to reproduce one copy or phonorecord from such fixation for archival purposes.

(2) Such regulations shall also provide standards and procedures by which the Register of Copyrights may make written demand, upon the owner of the right of transmission in the United States, for the deposit of a copy or phonorecord of a specific transmission program. Such deposit may, at the option of the owner of the right of transmission in the United States, be accomplished by gift, by loan for purposes of reproduction, or by sale at a price not to exceed the cost of reproducing and supplying the copy or phonorecord. The regulations established under this clause shall provide reasonable periods of not less than three months for compliance with a demand, and shall allow for extensions of such periods and adjustments in the scope of the demand or the methods for fulfilling it, as reasonably warranted by the circumstances. Willful failure or refusal to comply with the conditions prescribed by such regulations shall subject the owner of the right of transmission in the United States to liability for an amount, not to exceed the cost of reproducing and supplying the copy or phonorecord in question, to be paid into a specially designated fund in the Library of Congress.

(3) Nothing in this subsection shall be construed to require the making or retention, for purposes of deposit, of any copy or phonorecord of an unpublished transmission program, the transmission of which occurs before the receipt of a specific written demand as provided by clause (2).

(4) No activity undertaken in compliance with regulations prescribed under clauses (1) and (2) of this subsection shall result in liability if intended solely to assist in the acquisition of copies or phonorecords under this subsection.

§ 408. Copyright registration in general

(a) Registration Permissive. — At any time during the subsistence of the first term of copyright in any published or unpublished work in which the copyright was secured before January 1, 1978, and during the subsistence of any copyright secured on or after that date, the owner of copyright or of any exclusive right in the work may obtain registration of the copyright claim by delivering to the Copyright Office the deposit specified by this section, together with the application and fee specified by sections 409 and YPERLINK"http://www.copyright.gov/title17/92chap7.html"\l"708"708. Such registration is not a condition of copyright protection.

(b) Deposit for Copyright Registration. — Except as provided by subsection (c), the material deposited for registration shall include —

(1) in the case of an unpublished work, one complete copy or phonorecord;

(2) in the case of a published work, two complete copies or phonorecords of the best edition;

(3) in the case of a work first published outside the United States, one complete copy or phonorecord as so published;

(4) in the case of a contribution to a collective work, one complete copy or phonorecord of the best edition of the collective work.

Copies or phonorecords deposited for the Library of Congress under section 407 may be used to satisfy the deposit provisions of this section, if they are accompanied by the prescribed application and fee, and by any additional identifying material that the Register may, by regulation, require. The Register shall also prescribe regulations establishing requirements under which copies or phonorecords acquired for the Library of Congress under subsection (e) of section 407, otherwise than by deposit, may be used to satisfy the deposit provisions of this section.

(c) Administrative Classification and Optional Deposit. —

(1) The Register of Copyrights is authorized to specify by regulation the administrative classes into which works are to be placed for purposes of deposit and registration, and the nature of the copies or phonorecords to be deposited in the various classes specified. The regulations may require or permit, for particular classes, the deposit of identifying material instead of copies or phonorecords, the deposit of only one copy or phonorecord where two would normally be required, or a single registration for a group of related works. This administrative classification of works has no significance with respect to the subject matter of copyright or the exclusive rights provided by this title.

(2) Without prejudice to the general authority provided under clause (1), the Register of Copyrights shall establish regulations specifically permitting a single registration for a group of works by the same individual author, all first published as contributions to periodicals, including newspapers, within a twelve-month period, on the basis of a single deposit, application, and registration fee, under the following conditions —

(A) if the deposit consists of one copy of the entire issue of the periodical, or of the entire section in the case of a newspaper, in which each contribution was first published; and

(B) if the application identifies each work separately, including the periodical containing it and its date of first publication.

(3) As an alternative to separate renewal registrations under subsection (a) of section 304, a single renewal registration may be made for a group of works by the same individual author, all first published as contributions to periodicals, including newspapers, upon the filing of a single application and fee, under all of the following conditions:

(A) the renewal claimant or claimants, and the basis of claim or claims under section 304(a), is the same for each of the works; and

(B) the works were all copyrighted upon their first publication, either through separate copyright notice and registration or by virtue of a general copyright notice in the periodical issue as a whole; and

(C) the renewal application and fee are received not more than twenty-eight or less than twenty-seven years after the thirty-first day of December of the calendar year in which all of the works were first published; and

(D) the renewal application identifies each work separately, including the periodical containing it and its date of first publication.

(d) Corrections and Amplifications. — The Register may also establish, by regulation, formal procedures for the filing of an application for supplementary registration, to correct an error in a copyright registration or to amplify the information given in a registration. Such application shall be accompanied by the fee provided by section 708, and shall clearly identify the registration to be corrected or amplified. The information contained in a supplementary registration augments but does not supersede that contained in the earlier registration.

(e) Published Edition of Previously Registered Work. — Registration for the first published edition of a work previously registered in unpublished form may be made even though the work as published is substantially the same as the unpublished version.

(f) Preregistration of Works Being Prepared for Commercial Distribution. —

(1) Rulemaking. — Not later than 180 days after the date of enactment of this subsection, the Register of Copyrights shall issue regulations to establish procedures for preregistration of a work that is being prepared for commercial distribution and has not been published.

(2) Class of works. — The regulations established under paragraph (1) shall permit preregistration for any work that is in a class of works that the Register determines has had a history of infringement prior to authorized commercial distribution.

(3) Application for registration. — Not later than 3 months after the first publication of a work preregistered under this subsection, the applicant shall submit to the Copyright Office-

(A) an application for registration of the work;

(B) a deposit; and

(C) the applicable fee.

(4) Effect of untimely application. — An action under this chapter for infringement of a work preregistered under this subsection, in a case in which the infringement commenced no later than 2 months after the first publication of the work, shall be dismissed if the items described in paragraph (3) are not submitted to the Copyright Office in proper form within the earlier of —

(A) 3 months after the first publication of the work; or

(B) 1 month after the copyright owner has learned of the infringement.

§ 409. Application for copyright registration

The application for copyright registration shall be made on a form prescribed by the Register of Copyrights and shall include —

(1) the name and address of the copyright claimant;

(2) in the case of a work other than an anonymous or pseudonymous work, the name and nationality or domicile of the author or authors, and, if one or more of the authors is dead, the dates of their deaths;

(3) if the work is anonymous or pseudonymous, the nationality or domicile of the author or authors;

(4) in the case of a work made for hire, a statement to this effect;

(5) if the copyright claimant is not the author, a brief statement of how the claimant obtained ownership of the copyright;

(6) the title of the work, together with any previous or alternative titles under which the work can be identified;

(7) the year in which creation of the work was completed;

(8) if the work has been published, the date and nation of its first publication;

(9) in the case of a compilation or derivative work, an identification of any preexisting work or works that it is based on or incorporates, and a brief, general statement of the additional material covered by the copyright claim being registered;

(10) in the case of a published work containing material of which copies are required by section 601 to be manufactured in the United States, the names of the persons or organizations who performed the processes specified by subsection (c) of section 601 with respect to that material, and the places where those processes were performed; and

(11) any other information regarded by the Register of Copyrights as bearing upon the preparation or identification of the work or the existence, ownership, or duration of the copyright.

If an application is submitted for the renewed and extended term provided for in section 304(a)(3)(A) and an original term registration has not been made, the Register may request information with respect to the existence, ownership, or duration of the copyright for the original term.

§ 410. Registration of claim and issuance of certificate

(a) When, after examination, the Register of Copyrights determines that, in accordance with the provisions of this title, the material deposited constitutes copyrightable subject matter and that the other legal and formal requirements of this title have been met, the Register shall register the claim and issue to the applicant a certificate of registration under the seal of the Copyright Office. The certificate shall contain the information given in the application, together with the number and effective date of the registration.

(b) In any case in which the Register of Copyrights determines that, in accordance with the provisions of this title, the material deposited does not constitute copyrightable subject matter or that the claim is invalid for any other reason, the Register shall refuse registration and shall notify the applicant in writing of the reasons for such refusal.

(c) In any judicial proceedings the certificate of a registration made before or within five years after first publication of the work shall constitute *prima facie* evidence of the validity of the copyright and of the facts stated in the certificate. The evidentiary weight to be accorded the certificate of a registration made thereafter shall be within the discretion of the court.

(d) The effective date of a copyright registration is the day on which an application, deposit, and fee, which are later determined by the Register of Copyrights or by a court of competent jurisdiction to be acceptable for registration, have all been received in the Copyright Office.

§ 411. Registration and infringement actions

(a) Except for an action brought for a violation of the rights of the author under section 106A(a), and subject to the provisions of subsection (b), no action for infringement of the copyright in any United States work shall be instituted until preregistration or registration of the copyright claim has been made in accordance with this title. In any case, however, where the deposit, application, and fee required for registration have been delivered to the Copyright Office in proper form and registration has been refused, the applicant is entitled to institute an action for infringement if notice thereof, with a copy of the complaint, is served on the Register of Copyrights. The Register may, at his or her option, become a party to the action with respect to the issue of registrability of the copyright claim by entering an appearance within sixty days after such service, but the Register's failure to become a party shall not deprive the court of jurisdiction to determine that issue.

(b) In the case of a work consisting of sounds, images, or both, the first fixation of which is made simultaneously with its transmission, the copyright owner may, either before or after such fixation takes place, institute an action for infringement under section 501, fully subject to the remedies provided by sections 502 through 506 and sections 509 and 510, if, in accordance with requirements that the Register of Copyrights shall prescribe by regulation, the copyright owner —

(1) serves notice upon the infringer, not less than 48 hours before such fixation, identifying the work and the specific time and source of its first transmission, and declaring an intention to secure copyright in the work; and

(2) makes registration for the work, if required by subsection (a), within three months after its first transmission.

§ 412. Registration as prerequisite to certain remedies for infringement

In any action under this title, other than an action brought for a violation of the rights of the author under section 106A(a), an action for infringement of the copyright of a work that has been preregistered under section 408(f) before the commencement of the infringement and that has an effective date of registration not later than the earlier of 3 months after the first publication of the work or 1 month after the copyright owner has learned of the infringement, or an action instituted under section 411(b), no award of statutory damages or of attorney's fees, as provided by sections 504 and 505, shall be made for —

(1) any infringement of copyright in an unpublished work commenced before the effective date of its registration; or

(2) any infringement of copyright commenced after first publication of the work and before the effective date of its registration, unless such registration is made within three months after the first publication of the work.

§ 502. Remedies for infringement: Injunctions

(a) Any court having jurisdiction of a civil action arising under this title may, subject to the provisions of section 1498 of title 28, grant temporary and final injunctions on such terms as it may deem reasonable to prevent or restrain infringement of a copyright.

(b) Any such injunction may be served anywhere in the United States on the person enjoined; it shall be operative throughout the United States and shall be enforceable, by proceedings in contempt or otherwise, by any United States court having jurisdiction of that person. The clerk of the court granting the injunction shall, when requested by any other court in which enforcement of the injunction is sought, transmit promptly to the other court a certified copy of all the papers in the case on file in such clerk's office.

§ 503. Remedies for infringement: Impounding and disposition of infringing articles

(a) At any time while an action under this title is pending, the court may order the impounding, on such terms as it may deem reasonable, of all copies or phonorecords claimed to have been made or used in violation of the copyright owner's exclusive rights, and of all plates, molds, matrices, masters, tapes, film negatives, or other articles by means of which such copies or phonorecords may be reproduced.

(b) As part of a final judgment or decree, the court may order the destruction or other reasonable disposition of all copies or phonorecords found to have been made or used in violation of the copyright owner's exclusive rights, and of all plates, molds, matrices, masters, tapes, film negatives, or other articles by means of which such copies or phonorecords may be reproduced.

§ 504. Remedies for infringement: Damages and profits

(a) In General. — Except as otherwise provided by this title, an infringer of copyright is liable for either —

(1) the copyright owner's actual damages and any additional profits of the infringer, as provided by subsection (b); or

(2) statutory damages, as provided by subsection (c).

(b) Actual Damages and Profits. — The copyright owner is entitled to recover the actual damages suffered by him or her as a result of the infringement, and any profits of the infringer that are attributable to the infringement and are not taken into account in computing the actual damages. In establishing the infringer's profits, the copyright owner is required to present proof only of the infringer's gross revenue, and the infringer is required to prove his or her deductible expenses and the elements of profit attributable to factors other than the copyrighted work.

(c) Statutory Damages. —

(1) Except as provided by clause (2) of this subsection, the copyright owner may elect, at any time before final judgment is rendered, to recover, instead of actual damages and profits, an award of statutory damages for all infringements involved in the action, with respect to any one work, for which any one infringer is liable individually, or for which any two or more infringers are liable jointly and severally, in a sum of not less than $750 or more than $30,000 as the court considers just. For the purposes of this subsection, all the parts of a compilation or derivative work constitute one work.

(2) In a case where the copyright owner sustains the burden of proving, and the court finds, that infringement was committed willfully, the court in its discretion may increase the award of statutory damages to a sum of not more than $150,000. In a case where the infringer sustains the burden of proving, and the court finds, that such infringer was not aware and had no reason to believe that his or her acts constituted an infringement of copyright, the court in its discretion may reduce the award of statutory damages to a sum of not less than $200. The court shall remit statutory damages in any case where an infringer believed and had reasonable grounds for believing that his or her use of the copyrighted work was a fair use under section 107, if the infringer was: (i) an employee or agent of a nonprofit educational institution, library, or archives acting within the scope of his or her employment who, or such institution, library, or archives itself, which infringed by reproducing the work in copies or phonorecords; or (ii) a public broadcasting entity which or a person who, as a regular part of the nonprofit activities of a public broadcasting entity (as defined in subsection (g) of section 118) infringed by performing a published nondramatic literary work or by reproducing a transmission program embodying a performance of such a work.

(3) (A) In a case of infringement, it shall be a rebuttable presumption that the infringement was committed willfully for purposes of determining relief if the violator, or a person acting in concert with the violator, knowingly provided or knowingly caused to be provided materially false contact information to a domain name registrar, domain name registry, or other domain name registration authority in registering, maintaining, or renewing a domain name used in connection with the infringement.

(B) Nothing in this paragraph limits what may be considered willful infringement under this subsection.

(C) For purposes of this paragraph, the term "domain name" has the meaning given that term in section 45 of the Act entitled "An Act to provide for the registration and protection of trademarks used in commerce, to carry out the provisions of certain international conventions, and for other purposes" approved July 5, 1946 (commonly referred to as the "Trademark Act of 1946"; 15 U.S.C. 1127).

(d) Additional Damages in Certain Cases. — In any case in which the court finds that a defendant proprietor of an establishment who claims as a defense that its activities were exempt under section 110(5) did not have reasonable grounds to believe that its use of a copyrighted work was exempt under such section, the plaintiff shall be entitled to, in addition to any award of damages under this section, an additional award of two times the amount of the license fee that the proprietor of the establishment concerned should have paid the plaintiff for such use during the preceding period of up to 3 years.

§ 505. Remedies for infringement: Costs and attorney's fees

In any civil action under this title, the court in its discretion may allow the recovery of full costs by or against any party other than the United States or an officer thereof. Except as otherwise provided by this title, the court may also award a reasonable attorney's fee to the prevailing party as part of the costs.

§ 506. Criminal offenses

(a) Criminal Infringement. —

(1) In general. — Any person who willfully infringes a copyright shall be punished as provided under section 2319 of title 18, if the infringement was committed —

(A) for purposes of commercial advantage or private financial gain;

(B) by the reproduction or distribution, including by electronic means, during any 180-day period, of 1 or more copies or phonorecords of 1 or more copyrighted works, which have a total retail value of more than $1,000; or

(C) by the distribution of a work being prepared for commercial distribution, by making it available on a computer network accessible to members of the public, if such person knew or should have known that the work was intended for commercial distribution.

(2) Evidence. — For purposes of this subsection, evidence of reproduction or distribution of a copyrighted work, by itself, shall not be sufficient to establish willful infringement of a copyright.

(3) Definition. — In this subsection, the term "work being prepared for commercial distribution" means —

(A) a computer program, a musical work, a motion picture or other audiovisual work, or a sound recording, if, at the time of unauthorized distribution —

(i) the copyright owner has a reasonable expectation of commercial distribution; and

(ii) the copies or phonorecords of the work have not been commercially distributed; or

(B) a motion picture, if, at the time of unauthorized distribution, the motion picture —

(i) has been made available for viewing in a motion picture exhibition facility; and

(ii) has not been made available in copies for sale to the general public in the United States in a format intended to permit viewing outside a motion picture exhibition facility.

(b) Forfeiture and Destruction. — When any person is convicted of any violation of subsection (a), the court in its judgment of conviction shall, in addition to the penalty therein prescribed, order the forfeiture and destruction or other disposition of all infringing copies or phonorecords and all implements, devices, or equipment used in the manufacture of such infringing copies or phonorecords.

(c) Fraudulent Copyright Notice. — Any person who, with fraudulent intent, places on any article a notice of copyright or words of the same purport that such person knows to be false, or who, with fraudulent intent, publicly distributes or imports for public distribution any article bearing such notice or words that such person knows to be false, shall be fined not more than $2,500.

(d) Fraudulent Removal of Copyright Notice. — Any person who, with fraudulent intent, removes or alters any notice of copyright appearing on a copy of a copyrighted work shall be fined not more than $2,500.

(e) False Representation. — Any person who knowingly makes a false representation of a material fact in the application for copyright registration provided for by section 409, or in any written statement filed in connection with the application, shall be fined not more than $2,500.

(f) Rights of Attribution and Integrity. — Nothing in this section applies to infringement of the rights conferred by section 106A(a).

§ 507. Limitations on actions

(a) Criminal Proceedings. — Except as expressly provided otherwise in this title, no criminal proceeding shall be maintained under the provisions of this title unless it is commenced within 5 years after the cause of action arose.

(b) Civil Actions. — No civil action shall be maintained under the provisions of this title unless it is commenced within three years after the claim accrued.

§ 509. Seizure and forfeiture

(a) All copies or phonorecords manufactured, reproduced, distributed, sold, or otherwise used, intended for use, or possessed with intent to use in violation of section 506 (a), and all plates, molds, matrices, masters, tapes, film negatives, or other articles by means of which such copies or phonorecords may be reproduced, and all electronic, mechanical, or other devices for manufacturing, reproducing, or assembling such copies or phonorecords may be seized and forfeited to the United States.

(b) The applicable procedures relating to

(i) the seizure, summary and judicial forfeiture, and condemnation of vessels, vehicles, merchandise, and baggage for violations of the customs laws contained in title 19,

(ii) the disposition of such vessels, vehicles, merchandise, and baggage or the proceeds from the sale thereof,

(iii) the remission or mitigation of such forfeiture,

(iv) the compromise of claims, and

(v) the award of compensation to informers in respect of such forfeitures, shall apply to seizures and forfeitures incurred, or alleged to have been incurred, under the provisions of this section, insofar as applicable and not inconsistent with the provisions of this section; except that such duties as are imposed upon any officer or employee of the Treasury Department or any other person with respect to the seizure and forfeiture of vessels, vehicles, merchandise, and baggage under the provisions of the customs laws contained in title 19 shall be performed with respect to seizure and forfeiture of all articles described in subsection (a) by such officers, agents, or other persons as may be authorized or designated for that purpose by the Attorney General.

www.ingramcontent.com/pod-product-compliance
Lightning Source LLC
Chambersburg PA
CBHW070158230526
45471CB00002B/722